LOOKING BACK AT BRITAIN

EDWARDIAN SUMMER

1900s

EDWARDIAN SUMMER

1900s

Tony Allan

CONTENTS

1900s IMAGE GALLERY

FRONT COVER: The Hon Mrs Assheton Harbord and the Hon Mrs Yorke wait to compete in the Balloon Hare & Hounds race at the Hurlingham Club in Fulham, in July 1909. Ladies were always made welcome at Hurlingham.

BACK COVER: A Bat bi-plane with a Mr Mines at the controls during Doncaster Flying Week, October 1909.

TITLE PAGE: Children on a crowded beach, c1900.

OPPOSITE: A motor car passing between two horse-drawn cabs, photographed from an unusual perspective in 1907.

FOLLOWING PAGES:

Huntsmen and hounds of the West Norfolk Hunt, photographed with the local gamekeeper at the end of the decade.

A picnic party in the picturesque setting of ruined Netley Abbey in Hampshire, c1900.

An Edwardian drink-seller on London's Cheapside offers his refreshing mix of sherbert and water to passing city workers.

Two young boys have a swimming lesson in the Thames at Wallingford in September 1906. Each boy is being helped along from the riverbank – and saved from sinking – by a harness and rope attached to a pole.

A NEW AGE DAWNS

Revellers celebrating New Year's Eve on 31 December, 1899, did so with more than the usual enthusiasm and trepidation. They were entering the new century with a sense that an era was passing. The Victorian Age, which had seen Britain rise to a pinnacle of imperial grandeur, was in its 63rd year. The Queen herself was 80 years old – older than any previous British monarch save for her grandfather George III, who had died aged 81. Few people could recollect a time when Victoria had not been on the throne, and as mortality crept upon her, they regarded the future with a vague sense of foreboding.

REGAL SPLENDOUR Queen Alexandra, Edward VII's Danish-born consort, in a formal portrait with her pageboys on the day of her husband's coronation.

SNAPSHOT OF THE NATION

On the surface, the British had little enough to fear. The past 100 years had been Britain's century, and no-one yet realised that the new one would belong to the USA. Victoria ruled over an empire on which the sun famously never set, and its bounds had continued to grow over the past 20 years as the nation took its share of the spoils from the European 'scramble for Africa'. In 1899 competing white claims to lands in the southern part of the continent had embroiled the country for a second time in war with the Boers, settlers of Dutch extraction. The British public, having expected a quick victory, were surprised when the hardy farmers took the military initiative, inflicting early reverses on British troops. But few people expected success to be long delayed.

Domestically, at first sight the situation seemed serene. In the long years of Victorian prosperity, Britain had experienced a sustained demographic boom. At the turn of the new century there were almost 37 million people in the United Kingdom, excluding Ireland, a figure that had nearly doubled since the first modern UK census of 1841, early in Victoria's reign. The continuing vogue for large families ensured that it was a young population, with more than 40 per cent of the total below the age of 20; the downside of this statistic lay in the continuing high toll of infant mortality, with one baby in eight dying before reaching its first birthday. Divorce remained a rarity, with fewer than a thousand decrees granted

TAKING THEIR EASE
Looked at retrospectively, the Edwardian era seemed to pass in a golden glow, leaving later generations with the impression that people spent the whole decade lazing about and having fun, like the group below enjoying a picnic near Hereford in 1901. Much of the nostalgia came from the stark contrast with the horrors of what was soon to come: the First World War and the trenches of the Western Front would blow the Edwardian way of life to smithereens. Yet for now, the quarter of the population who did not have to live by manual labour enjoyed standards that were genuinely comfortable. For this minority, income tax rates of 5 per cent and the ready availability of low-paid servants were a recipe for the good life.

IN THE BACKSTREETS

For the urban poor, life was a far cry from the ease of the leisured classes. Skilled workers with secure jobs enjoyed home comforts and a respectable lifestyle, but millions of other city-dwellers struggled to make any kind of living at all. Not everyone succeeded; at a time when the only welfare was provided by the Poor Law and the workhouse, pioneering sociological studies showed that between a quarter and a third of the entire population of Britain regularly went hungry. Overcrowding was another problem. In London's East End, where this photograph was taken, a third of the population lived in accommodation housing more than two people to a room. Even here, however, there were positive aspects to city life in Edwardian times: in particular, the low crime rate and strong sense of community meant that children mostly played in the street without fear.

each year, although this reflected the complexity, expense and general unacceptability of divorce rather than the national state of marital contentment. Crime levels were extraordinarily low, with only 300 offences recorded for every 100,000 people; by the end of the 20th century – when admittedly police record-keeping was vastly more comprehensive – the figure was approaching 9,000.

The urban drift

Victoria's reign had seen an ongoing drift from the countryside. In 1871, almost two-thirds of the population had lived in communities of less than 50,000 – small country towns or villages, for the most part. Thirty years later the situation had been reversed, with roughly two-thirds now living in cities. Some 13 million people were crammed into the five largest conurbations, of which the biggest was Greater London, the largest city in the world, with almost 7 million inhabitants.

The people in the great urban agglomerations were rigidly divided on class lines. Almost three-quarters of the population earned their living as manual workers – a figure that would be halved by the end of the century. More than 2 million women were employed in domestic service, along with half a million men. Life at the bottom of the pile was grim indeed. Social researchers estimated that almost one third of the population lived in poverty, earning too little to feed themselves to adequate nutritional standards, let alone to enjoy the wider amenities of life. The result was widespread sickliness and infirmity, which became all too evident to the authorities during the Boer War: out of the 20,000 men who volunteered to fight, some 6,000 were rejected as unfit for military service.

For a minority of the population, life could be very good indeed. The rich lived magnificently, exuding a showy opulence that marked them out as the chosen elite of the world's greatest power. The aristocracy enjoyed almost regal splendour, while even middle-class families had servants to look after them. One typical office administrator, the secretary to the board of directors of an iron and shipping works in Jarrow, kept a cook, a housemaid, two other maids and a governess for his children. The lower middle classes clung to the skirts of privilege by nurturing a cult of respectability that distinguished them from the working masses. One Islington resident recalled for an oral historian how his father, a Post Office clerk with a young family, always took particular care to be well groomed. 'He wore a bowler hat and never wore shabby clothes. He never worked in his shirt sleeves and there were no Christian names used at work.'

Deceptive appearances

To the casual observer, then, the late Victorian world was settled and secure, but the more thoughtful of Britain's citizens regarded the future with a certain apprehension, even anxiety. There was a feeling that many of the pillars on which the social framework rested were being gradually undermined. True, Britain remained the world's greatest economic power, but it was being challenged; Germany and the USA had both grown faster than Britain in industrial might since 1870. The countryside was in a state of decline, with cheap imported American grain undercutting British wheat and refrigerated meat and dairy products coming in from Argentina, Australia, New Zealand and northern Europe. Even the family, that great bulwark of Victorian values, was no longer what it had been. The birth-rate had been falling, and the typical number of children had declined from the five or six of earlier times to a mere three or four, causing concerns that Britain was slipping behind the prolific Germans in demographic terms too.

LONG SHE REIGNED OVER US
Seen here in 1900, at the age of 80, Queen Victoria had already become the longest-reigning British monarch. By the time of her death in January 1901 she had been on the throne for 63 years, 7 months and 2 days – more than 4 years longer than the previous record-holder, George III. She had outlived two sons and one daughter; another would die later the same year. In her last years Victoria spent much of her time either at Osborne House on the Isle of Wight or at Balmoral in the Scottish Highlands. The contrast with her successor, the extrovert Edward VII, could hardly have been greater.

A NATION MOURNS

Against all such worries the abiding presence of the Queen seemed a reassuring counterweight. The heartfelt celebrations that greeted her Diamond Jubilee in 1897 had demonstrated the depth of the public's affection. So stories of her declining strength were met with alarm. A pall of gloom fell over the nation on 22 January, 1901, when news spread that the Queen was dead.

As was her custom, Victoria had gone to Osborne House on the Isle of Wight for the Christmas holidays. It was there, at 6.30 in the evening, that she finally succumbed to a cerebral haemorrhage. She was attended at her bedside not just by her eldest son Edward but also by her eldest grandson, Kaiser Wilhelm II of Germany, who was holding her hand when she passed away.

'I felt her death far more than I should have expected. She was a sustaining symbol and the wild waters are upon us now.'

Henry James, writer

In accordance with her wishes, Victoria was laid to rest dressed in white and wearing her wedding veil. She had left instructions, too, on the contents of her coffin, including her beloved husband Albert's dressing gown and a photograph of her longtime favourite, the Scots ghillie John Brown, which was placed in her left hand. Her funeral – a military affair, with the coffin drawn through London by eight white and bay horses – was attended by most of Europe's ruling elite, the kings of Greece and Portugal, five crown princes and 14 princes among them.

In the East End of London, working people showed their grief in the traditional way. 'Even poor little houses that faced onto the street put a board up and painted it black,' one observer recalled. 'All the shops had black shutters up, and everyone felt as if they'd lost somebody.' Up and down the country people sensed that an era had ended and speculated on what the new reign might bring.

FINAL JOURNEY
Queen Victoria died at Osborne House on 22 January, 1901. After lying in state there for ten days, her body was carried across the Solent to Portsmouth in the royal yacht *Alberta*, sailing between two 5-mile-long lines of warships, which fired their guns at one-minute intervals throughout the voyage. From Portsmouth the coffin was carried by train to Victoria Station, then in horse-drawn procession through the streets to Paddington to allow the public to say a final farewell; almost a million people travelled to London for the occasion. In Paddington a second train was waiting to take Victoria to Windsor, where a team of sailors pulled the hearse up to the castle for the private funeral – the horses originally envisaged for the job proved too skittish. The white wreath on the front of the royal locomotive below was in accordance with Victoria's own wishes; she had come to dislike mourning black.

INTO THE EDWARDIAN ERA

One reason for concern on the Queen's death was the character of the new king. Edward was 59 years old, and his past life had been touched by more than a whiff of scandal. Some of the nation's best minds regarded his accession with disquiet. Rudyard Kipling called him a 'corpulent voluptuary'. The novelist Henry James wrote to a friend that the nation had 'dropped to Edward … fat Edward … Edward the Caresser', adding 'I mourn the safe, motherly old middle-class queen who held the nation warm under the folds of her big, hideous, Scotch-plaid shawl.'

Worries about Edward's temperament had started early in his life. The second child and eldest son born to Victoria and Albert, he grew up in the shadow of the

Queen's adored husband. Christened Albert Edward after his father, he was always known within the royal family as 'Bertie'. To train him for his future role Victoria entrusted his upbringing to a succession of disciplinarian tutors. He quickly proved a disappointment. Victoria privately dismissed him as having 'a small, empty brain', while Albert confided in a letter to a friend that 'I never in my life met with such a thorough and cunning lazybones'. Having failed to distinguish himself as a student first at Oxford and then Cambridge universities, Edward spent a brief spell on manoeuvres with the army in Ireland, where fellow officers hid an actress in his tent – a jape that backfired badly when his mother got to hear of it.

In the vain hope of forestalling further sexual escapades, he was encouraged at the age of 21 to marry Alexandra, daughter of King Christian IX of Denmark, whose relatively austere upbringing recommended her to Victoria as a suitable consort for her son. Beautiful, kindly and high-spirited, the young princess proved indeed to be a dignified and supportive partner to whom Edward remained deeply attached for the rest of his life. Yet the genuine affection he felt for Alexandra did nothing to inhibit his pursuit of extra-marital adventures. There was a scandal in 1869 when Sir Charles Mordaunt, a wealthy country squire and Member of Parliament, threatened to cite Edward as a co-respondent in a divorce case. His wife Harriet was just one of a string of society beauties whose names were linked with the high-living prince, among them the actress Lillie Langtry, the singer Hortense Schneider, and the eccentric Daisy, Countess of Warwick, who ended her days as a convert to socialism. Most famously of all, Edward was long involved with Alice Keppel, wife of a complaisant aristocrat and remembered today as a

PLAYBOY PRINCE
Edward VII's accession saw a sea change in the image of the British monarchy. Where his mother was the incarnation of respectability, the pleasure-loving prince surrounded himself with a social set that enthusiastically embraced horse-racing, gambling and a constant round of house parties. He is pictured above decorously shaking a leg with other guests at Mar Lodge near Braemar in the Highlands. Such gatherings allowed Edward plenty of opportunities to rendezvous with a long succession of mistresses, of whom Alice Keppel (left) was the best-known. Edward's other passions included motor-cars; he is seen here (right) seated alongside the future Lord Montagu of Beaulieu, a leading pioneer of the automobile age, in Montagu's 12-horsepower Daimler.

grandmother of Camilla, Duchess of Cornwall. Edward's relationship with this beautiful socialite was sufficiently well-known to prompt Winston Churchill, a rising young politician at the time of Edward's accession, to ask ironically in a letter to a friend, 'Will the Keppel be appointed First Lady of the Bedchamber?'

By the time of Edward's marriage to Alexandra, his father Albert was already dead and the Prince was heir to the throne, much to the alarm of his widowed mother, who considered him too frivolous to handle affairs of state. 'What will become of the country if I die?' Victoria privately mused. 'If Bertie succeeds, he would spend his life in one whirl of amusements.' As heir apparent for four decades, Edward did much to justify his mother's fears. The Marlborough House set, named after his London residence, gained a reputation for high living. Their behaviour came into the public spotlight in the Royal Baccarat Scandal of 1891, which led to Edward being called to give evidence in court as a witness in a libel trial. Even though he himself was not accused of wrongdoing, his behaviour attracted widespread criticism.

Edward's day finally comes

There were legitimate reasons, then, for Victoria's concern, and on his accession events did not seem to augur well for the new reign. His coronation, set for 5 July, 1902, had to be delayed when he suffered a life-threatening bout of appendicitis, and he was not formally crowned until August. The ceremony itself was saved from disaster in the most unlikely circumstances when the Master of Horse, who was responsible for getting the royal party safely to Westminster Abbey, had a

STREET PARTY
Despite Victoria's fears, Edward proved immediately popular when he came to the throne, appealing to a public weary of the high moral tone of the old Queen's reign. By the time of his coronation, which was delayed until the summer of 1902 to allow a suitable time for mourning as well as for making the necessary arrangements, he was already firmly established in the nation's affections. The decorations enlivening London thoroughfares for the ceremony, like Queen Victoria Street (below), reflected a genuine mood of national rejoicing. It helped that, as J B Priestley noted, Edward 'enjoyed being a king'. He took genuine pleasure in public appearances, not least at the racecourse, where that year his horse Sceptre won four classics – the St Leger, the Oaks, and the 1000 and 2000 Guineas. By the time of the actual coronation, the King was being familiarly toasted in pubs and clubs as 'Good Old Teddie!'.

6582.

CROWNED HEAD

Although Edward cultivated a less formal, more approachable manner than his mother as ruler of Britain, he remained a stickler for etiquette. He would have felt very much at ease, then, in his coronation robes. Those who failed to share his dress sense sometimes suffered when they got it wrong; he once refused to allow an aide to accompany him to an art exhibition because he was wearing a tailcoat, commenting 'I thought everyone must know that a short jacket is always worn with a silk hat at a private view in the morning'. In this formal portrait Edward is shown wearing the Crown of St Edward, said to be based on that worn by Edward the Confessor in the 11th century. The lighter Imperial State Crown was used in the actual ceremony.

premonitory dream. In it he saw the carriage becoming stuck in the arch separating Horse Guards Parade from Whitehall. Subsequent investigation revealed that resurfacing of the roadway during Victoria's long reign had indeed reduced the clearance to some 2 feet (60cm) below the required level. Urgent road repairs were undertaken to allow the carriage to pass freely.

Presages notwithstanding, something unexpected happened once Edward eventually reached the throne. Invested with the aura of royalty, the scapegrace prince started to exude a benignly avuncular presence. Abandoning his first name Albert, with all its loaded associations, he chose to reign as Edward – a change that signalled a more general willingness to turn his back on his mother's legacy.

SCENES FROM EDWARD VII'S CORONATION

Edward's coronation was originally planned for July 1902, as indicated on the dinner invitation (right). Royalty duly flocked to London from across Europe and beyond, only to be disappointed. Shortly before the intended date the King became acutely ill with appendicitis and the ceremony had to be postponed. Most of the foreign guests returned home and the banquet was cancelled, providing an unexpected bounty for London's East End. As the royal chef later wrote, 'It was the poor of Whitechapel and not the foreign kings, princes and diplomats who had the *consommé de faisan aux quenelles*, the *côtelette de bécassines à la Souvaroff* and many other dishes ...'.

When the coronation eventually took place, on 9 August, the event was primarily a domestic affair. Even so, it was celebrated with all the pomp and circumstance befitting a ruler who bore the titles Emperor of India and King of the United Kingdom and Dominions. Indian military representatives played a part in the rearranged ceremonies; some of them are seen here (top right) on the terrace of the Houses of Parliament with the Conservative MP for Oxford, Arthur Annesley, 11th Viscount Valentia.

Following long-established tradition, the coronation ceremony took place in Westminster Abbey, a so-called 'Royal Peculiar' directly under the jurisdiction of the monarch, rather than in a cathedral. Church dignitaries are seen above carrying the Bible, crown and sceptre to the Abbey. An unusual – and at the time unpublicised – feature of the event was the provision of a special box within the Abbey for various lady friends of the king, including Alice Keppel; court wags dubbed it the 'Loose Box'.

For Edward's subjects, the first coronation in 65 years was something to celebrate. Londoners filled the streets to enjoy the spectacle of the royal procession to the Abbey (far right). The event also left an enduring legacy in the anthem 'Land of Hope and Glory', which first saw the light of day as Edward's 'Coronation Ode'.

Her beloved Osborne House was given to the Navy as a training college, and Edward abandoned her custom of teatime receptions in favour of evening courts.

In some ways Edward's style of kingship confirmed his mother's worst fears. His annual round was a constant cycle of pleasures, interspersed only when necessary with the expected regal duties. Christmas and the New Year were spent at Sandringham House in Norfolk, followed by a week's shooting in the country before the King returned to London for the State Opening of Parliament, then held in February. In early March Edward set out for Paris and Biarritz, followed perhaps by a cruise in the royal yacht. He was back in England by May, in time to preside over the London season, including such highlights as the Ascot and Goodwood race meetings and the June presentation of the year's crop of debutantes. At the start of August he was on the yacht again for the Cowes Regatta, after which it was time for his annual cure at Marienbad, a spa in Bohemia. Then there was a short stay in London, followed by Doncaster race week, with shooting and stalking at Balmoral in the month of October. The closing months of the year were divided between Buckingham Palace, Sandringham and Windsor.

Edward's subjects, then, were never under any illusions but that he liked to enjoy himself. Yet his hedonism suited the spirit of the times. Far from disapproving, as Victoria had feared, people came to see Edward as a reassuringly human figure whose taste for the comforts of life mirrored their own, albeit on a grander, more luxurious scale. Genial and good-hearted, this new Merry Monarch became identified with his time; the 1900s would be remembered as the Edwardian Era, a compliment that none of his immediate successors would share.

> Edward became 'the most popular king England had known since the early 1660s, the first years of Charles II's Restoration'.
>
> J B Priestley, writer

UNFINISHED BUSINESS – THE SECOND BOER WAR

The political system that the King found himself presiding over was something less than a democracy, at least by present-day standards. Barely a third of the adult population had the vote – more precisely, some two-thirds of the men and none of the women. The unelected House of Lords, mostly hereditary peers, had almost as much legislative power as the elected House of Commons, having the ability to reject bills approved by the lower house (although convention demanded that it should not exercise that right in respect of the Chancellor's annual budget). As one Liberal wit put it: 'The House of Lords represent nobody but themselves, and they enjoy the full confidence of their constituents.'

Edward also inherited Victoria's last Prime Minister, the bearded, myopic Lord Salisbury, who was already 70 years old and six years into his third term of

HIGH TORY

Lord Salisbury, Queen Victoria's last prime minister, stares pugnaciously at the camera for an informal portrait taken in 1900. By the turn of the century, the 70-year-old Conservative had been a Member of Parliament for 47 years and was in the midst of his third term in the nation's highest office, having first been appointed premier as head of a short-lived ministry in 1885. Born into the aristocracy and educated at Eton and Christ Church, Oxford, Salisbury fitted the traditional image of the Tory grandee. He led his party to victory in the Khaki Election of 1900 and remained in office until July 1902, steering the nation through the first 18 months of Edward VII's reign. Yet his last years in power were unhappy ones personally; half-blind and in failing health, he bitterly missed his wife of 42 years, who had died in 1899.

CITIZEN ARMY

Britain's opponents in the Second Boer War were unconventional fighters (left). They had no standing army, no uniforms and no formal military training. Instead, all men and boys over the age of 14 – for the most part farmers and smallholders – were required to fight, bringing their own arms and horses with them. Nevertheless, they were skilled marksmen and they also had the advantage of modern weapons shipped in from Europe, mainly from Germany, in the years before the war. They used commando-style tactics, employing small groups of snipers to divert attention from their main forces, and proved masters of camouflage. It was in response to this that the British forces adopted khaki rather than the traditional scarlet uniforms, which made them easy targets in the veldt. In the first months of the war the Boers took the initiative in the fighting and had considerable success. Below, a crowd of onlookers turn out to watch a trainload of British prisoners of war arriving in the Boer capital, Pretoria.

office. An aristocratic Conservative of the old school, he regarded his chief field of expertise as foreign policy. He had been an architect of the 'splendid isolation' that had seen Britain avoid entanglements with Continental allies in favour of the unencumbered pursuit of its own imperial ambitions. It was fitting, then, that the great matter of Salisbury's final term was a colonial conflict.

Unlike most of the imperial ventures of Victoria's reign, the Boer War was fought against opponents of European origin. The Boers were white farmers, mostly from Dutch or German ethnic backgrounds, who had been contesting control of southern Africa with the British for centuries past. The immediate cause of hostilities lay in Her Majesty's government's support for mainly British migrant workers who had flocked to the autonomous Boer republic of the Transvaal following the discovery of gold and diamonds there in the 1880s. The dispute over the civil rights of these *uitlanders* (foreign immigrants) offered convenient cover for British ambitions to incorporate the mineral-rich Transvaal and its sister republic, the Orange Free State, within a British-dominated federation. When negotiations came to nothing, the two sides went to war.

The British under siege

In the first months of the fighting, the Boer forces surprised their powerful opponents by taking the offensive, and soon substantial British forces were cooped up under siege in the towns of Mafeking, Kimberley and Ladysmith, all within Britain's imperial territory. Initial attempts to relieve the garrisons resulted in

TROOP SURGE
The response to early setbacks in the war was to send out more troops. By January 1900, 180,000 men had been assembled from all corners of the Empire, the largest array of fighting men Britain had ever sent overseas. Troops under the command of Lord Methuen – seen above in action at Honey Nest Kloof – drove north toward Mafeking, encountering heavy resistance on the way. When the town was finally relieved on 17 May, 1900, the news (left) triggered widespread rejoicing across Britain.

significant British defeats, notably at Colenso and Spion Kop, and it was only after massive reinforcements arrived in early 1900 that the tide of battle began to turn.

Kimberley was the first siege to be lifted, on 15 February, 1900, followed by Ladysmith on 28 February; both had stood firm for four months. The news was greeted with rejoicing back in Britain, but when Mafeking was finally relieved – on 17 May, after holding out pluckily for 217 days – the British public reacted with almost hysterical joy. A new word, 'mafficking', was coined to describe the scenes of jubilation in all the major cities. The garrison's commander, Colonel Robert Baden-Powell, became a national hero. Further successes followed, and by late 1900 the Orange Free State had been annexed and imperial troops had marched into the Transvaal's capital, Pretoria.

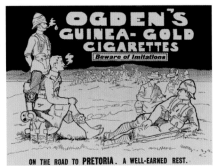
THE ROAD TO PRETORIA
Early in 1900 a new commander arrived in South Africa to direct the British war effort. Field Marshal Lord Roberts (left) was a 67-year-old veteran of many campaigns. He had won the Victoria Cross 41 years earlier for gallantry in the Indian Mutiny and had also seen active service in Afghanistan. He was able to use the vastly increased troop numbers available to him to turn the tide of battle, forcing the surrender of the Boer general Piet Cronje with 4,000 men at Paardeberg before moving on to capture Bloemfontein, capital of the Orange Free State. The road then lay open to Pretoria. Although the going was not quite as easy as suggested by the cigarette advertisement at bottom left, Boer resistance by then had been largely broken. After brushing aside a force of 800 marksmen at the Zand River (right), the British entered the capital unopposed on 5 June, 1900. Roberts subsequently saw fit to declare the war over – prematurely, as it turned out, for a whole new phase was about to begin with the opposing Boer forces adopting guerrilla tactics.

Premature peace

The British commander, Field Marshal Lord Roberts, felt satisfied enough to declare the war over. One consequence of the change in fortune was an upsurge in patriotic support for the government of the day back in Britain. In the 'Khaki Election' that took place in autumn 1900, Salisbury's Conservatives – often referred to at the time as 'Unionists' because of their alliance over the previous 15 years with defecting Liberal Unionists opposed to Irish Home Rule – were convincingly returned to power for a fresh term in office, although with a marginally reduced majority over the opposition Liberal Party. Conditions seemed set fair for a swift end to hostilities and for the subsequent incorporation of the troublesome Boer farmers into an expanded British imperium.

The Boers thought otherwise. Although their armies had been defeated, their resistance was not and they continued to wage a bitter guerrilla campaign in the southern African countryside that dragged on for another couple of years. In response, the British army brought in Lord Kitchener, who had avenged the death of Gordon with victory at Omdurman in the Sudan, to take over from Roberts.

continued on page 38

BIG GUNS

Artillery played a significant role in the Boer War. In the years leading up to the hostilities the Boers had imported 100 of the latest Krupp field guns from Germany and also some siege guns from France. The British forces had high hopes of their own weapons, particularly of the 4.7-inch naval gun shown here at the moment of actual firing. The gun was nicknamed 'Joe Chamberlain' after Britain's colonial secretary, an ardent advocate of the imperial cause. Yet 'Old Joey', as it became familiarly known, was less effective in battle than had been hoped, largely because of Boer diversionary tactics; groups of snipers would set out to attract the gun's fire, while larger troop concentrations waited unseen and undisturbed in trenches nearby. The photograph shows 'Old Joey' in action in early 1900 near Magersfontein on the road to Kimberley.

BEHIND BRITISH LINES

Learning from the mistakes of the Crimean War, the British army was better equipped to cope with battlefield casualties in the Boer conflict than it had been in Florence Nightingale's day. The Royal Army Medical Corps, which had been set up the year before the Boer War started, provided officers and men to staff field hospitals where battlefield casualties were treated (right). They were helped by volunteer nurses and stretcher-bearers; among the ranks of the latter was the young Mohandas Gandhi, who was working in Durban at the time as a lawyer. In all, some 22,000 soldiers were treated for wounds over the course of the war. Disease proved a greater menace than the fighting, accounting for more than twice as many deaths. Spread by crowded and insanitary living conditions – the two soldiers mending cavalry equipment below were relatively well housed – dysentery and enteric fever took a terrible toll, not least in tented hospitals like this one (left), set up with Boer permission outside Ladysmith to treat the sick and wounded of the besieged town.

Britain's concentration camp shame

Kitchener introduced a savage scorched-earth policy designed to deprive the fighters of local support, burning farmsteads and forcibly moving wives and children into tented internment centres – concentration camps. Overcrowded and underfunded, the camps became breeding grounds of malnutrition and epidemic disease. In all, some 26,000 Boer women and children were to die in these concentration centres, and several thousand more black Africans succumbed as prisoners in separate camps.

Although Kitchener's tactics proved militarily effective, they were hugely controversial. The war had always been regarded with hostility abroad, where it was seen as a land-grab engineered by British imperialists eager to get their hands on the Transvaal gold and diamonds. The Boers' political leader, President Paul Kruger, received a hero's welcome when he travelled to Europe in search of diplomatic support. For a time Britain was so unpopular on the Continent that Edward VII had to abandon plans to visit the Paris Universal Exhibition of 1900 for fear of the hostile reception he could expect.

Divided opinions

Public opinion in Britain became aroused when reports on conditions in the camps began to circulate, largely thanks to the investigations of the welfare campaigner Emily Hobhouse. Soon the nation was divided between supporters of the war and protesters eager to bring it to a speedy end. The opposition Liberal Party took up the anti-war cause under the inspiration of a fiery young radical MP

BITTER EXILE
The British military authorities had considerable difficulty knowing what to do with the thousands of prisoners they took in the course of the war. Fearing that prison camps in the occupied lands would be obvious targets for raiders seeking to set the captives free, they sought alternative solutions. At first ships were used as temporary internment centres. When that expedient proved insufficient, the next step was to send captured fighters abroad. Some 5,000 men and boys, including the Boer general Piet Cronje, were despatched to St Helena, the tiny mid-Atlantic island where Napoleon's life had ended. A similar number were sent to Ceylon (now Sri Lanka), and smaller contingents to other parts of the Indian subcontinent; the group above were photographed at Kakul in what is now Pakistan. In the later stages of the war, non-combatant civilians were herded into concentration camps – a term newly minted at the time – to prevent them from offering support to the guerrilla fighters; many thousands died of epidemic diseases.

QUEST FOR AN ELUSIVE PEACE
Despite British expectations of a quick settlement after the fall of Pretoria, the war dragged on for another couple of years. The Boers could no longer muster sufficient forces to confront their opponents in pitched battle, but they were not prepared to concede. Instead, they drew on their superior knowledge of local terrain and adopted guerrilla tactics, raiding supply lines and attacking isolated outposts. British commanders found it hard to counter these mobile raiders. Eventually more than 50,000 troops were committed to manning a network of fortified blockhouses, each one designed to house from six to eight guards. At the same time the British made overtures to the Boer commanders, offering peace terms that were initially rejected. The Boer and British leaders met for the first time in March 1901 to discuss a settlement (below); Kitchener is seated second from right.

'When is a war not a war? When it is carried on by methods of barbarism in south Africa.'

Sir Henry Campbell-Bannerman, Liberal Party leader, June 1901

from north Wales, David Lloyd George. The mild-mannered party leader, Sir Henry Campbell-Bannerman, left no doubt that Lloyd George had his full support.

The divisions splitting the nation came to the boil that December when Lloyd George was invited to address an anti-war rally in Birmingham. The city was the political stronghold of Joseph Chamberlain, a passionate advocate of empire whose defection to the Conservatives 15 years earlier over the issue of Irish Home Rule had split the Liberal Party and lost them power. Now, Lloyd George's presence in the city was seen as a slap in the face by the pro-war lobby. Chamberlain himself privately commented that 'If Ll G wants his life, he had better keep away from Birmingham … If he doesn't go, I will see that it is known that he is afraid. If he does go, he will deserve all he gets.'

continued on page 43

ANTI-WAR CRUSADER

When this portrait was taken in the early 1900s, David Lloyd George was the most controversial politician in Britain. For his admirers, he was the voice of all those who opposed the conduct of the Boer War and someone who dared to tell the truth about British policy and actions in South Africa. For his detractors, notably the supporters of the pro-imperial Joseph Chamberlain, he was little better than a traitor – a man who had stated publicly, 'We have now taken to killing babies'.

Lloyd George was born to Welsh parents in Manchester in 1863 and was brought up a Welsh-speaker in North Wales, with English as his second language. He was elected to the Liberal benches of the House of Commons at the age of 27, and soon attracted attention through his energy and eloquence. His anti-war stance brought him national prominence, and when the Liberals returned to power in 1906 he served in the Cabinet first as President of the Board of Trade and, from 1908 on, as Chancellor of the Exchequer. He became Prime Minister during the First World War and remains the only Welshman to have held the office.

VICTORY CELEBRATION

On 31 May, 1902, crowds stretch as far as the eye can see in the City of London to celebrate the end of the Boer War. By the terms of the Treaty of Vereeniging, signed that day, Britain annexed the two formerly independent Boer republics – the South African Republic and the Orange Free State – which thus became part of the British Empire. But victory came at a high price. Over 6,000 British troops had been killed in battle, and more than twice that number had died of disease; Boer civilians had suffered even more heavily. In cash terms, the war had cost over £200 million, a huge sum at the time.

On the night Birmingham's town hall was packed with Chamberlain loyalists ready for trouble. The Welsh orator got no further into his speech than the first few sentences, in which he protested at the Union Jack, 'the pride and property of our common country', being turned instead 'into Mr Chamberlain's pocket handkerchief'. That was enough, and the crowd stormed the stage. Lloyd George was smuggled out of a back door disguised in a policeman's uniform. In the ensuing fighting two people, one of them a police constable, were killed.

The end at last

The war finally ended in May 1902 with the surrender of the last Boer guerrillas and the signing of the Treaty of Vereeniging. The Boer republics ceased to exist as independent entities and the Union of South Africa was born. For Britain it had been an expensive victory: almost 20,000 soldiers had been lost to disease or military action, and it now agreed to provide some £3 million in reconstruction funds. And just seven years later, the Boer republics would win a new constitution and a return to limited self-government. The settlement at least healed the rift between pro and anti-war factions at home. The rest of the decade was to be a time of peace, in which the clash between conservatives and progressives would be fought instead over domestic social issues.

ANTICIPATING THE FUTURE

In 1901 a rising young author greeted the new century with an extraordinary work of prophecy. Thirty-four years old at the time, H G Wells had already established a reputation as a science-fiction pioneer with such novels as *The Time Machine, The Invisible Man* and *The War of the Worlds*. Now, in a work called *Anticipations of the Reaction of Mechanical and Scientific Progress upon Human Life and Thought,* he set out his vision of the world as it might be in the year 2000. Today, the book is remembered, if at all, mainly for a final section apparently advocating euthanasia for social undesirables, among them chronic alcoholics and those afflicted with incurable transmissible diseases. Yet the earlier parts of the book contain an extraordinarily prescient vision of the way in which the 20th-century world, and Britain in particular, would develop under the influence of technological change. *Anticipations* shows how the future looked to an unusually far-sighted individual as the Victorian era came to an end.

PROPHETIC VOICE

H G Wells (right) was born in 1866, the son of a professional cricketer renowned for his fast bowling whose career was prematurely ended by a fractured thigh. The family was thrown back on the resources of a sporting goods and chinaware shop that they owned in Bromley High Street, but the business never prospered. Financial hardship eventually forced his parents to apprentice the future novelist to a draper at the age of 15. Two years later, Wells escaped his life of drudgery there thanks to a scholarship which enabled him to pursue his education in London; one of his teachers was the Darwinian scientist T H Huxley. After a time spent teaching, Wells turned to writing to earn his living, rising to prominence as the author of a series of futuristic novels beginning with *The Time Machine* (1895). From the start his concern was with the future development of society. In his 1899 novel *When the Sleeper Wakes* (below), Wells imagined a protagonist who emerged from a 200-year slumber to find that, through inherited wealth invested in a trust, he had come to own the world.

A world of mobility

One of Wells's most inspired insights was to realise, at the dawn of the automobile era, how profoundly the new development would affect the future world. He foresaw that motor vehicles powered by 'explosive engines' employing gas or petrol would finally put an end to the 19th-century 'Age of Coal and Steam'. At a time when legislation still limited cars to 12 miles per hour, he predicted the coming of motor trucks carrying goods in bulk, motor buses replacing the horse-drawn omnibuses and carriages of his time, and 'hired or privately owned motor carriages' capable of travelling 300 miles or more in a day. These wonders would travel on roads exclusively reserved for motor transport, surfaced with 'very good asphalt sloped to drain', that would cross one another by means of flyovers and underpasses to combat the risk of congestion at junctions.

Extending his vision to the social effects of the new mobility, he foresaw not just the outward spread of cities but also the development of long-distance commuting, forecasting that 'it is not too much to say that the London citizen of the year 2000 AD may have a choice of nearly all England and Wales south of Nottingham and east of Exeter as his suburb'. In time, Wells predicted, all Britain short of the Scottish Highlands would come to be linked in a single, loose urban region, criss-crossed with telephone poles and, regrettably, advertising hoardings and dotted with wooded areas and 'islands of agriculture'. The boundaries between city and country life would fade until 'to receive the daily paper a few hours late, to wait a day or so for goods one has ordered will be the extreme measure of rusticity'.

PUBLIC TRANSPORTS OF DELIGHT
The 1900s were marked by revolutionary progress in the field of transport. Besides witnessing the birth of aviation and a vast expansion in car ownership, the decade saw a massive reduction in the number of horse-drawn vehicles on city streets. Hansom cabs gave way to motor taxis, while buses and trams mostly abandoned horsepower in favour of new forms of locomotion. The first petrol-powered omnibuses made their appearance in London in 1902. After a few brief, unsatisfactory experiments with steam power, trams turned to electrification. The first British city to replace its horse-drawn trams with electric models was Hull, in 1899. Croydon followed in 1901, and two years later the London County Council Tramways opened its first electric line between Westminster Bridge and Tooting. Crowds turned out to watch the opening ceremony, when the Prince of Wales – the future King George V – briefly took the controls (right).

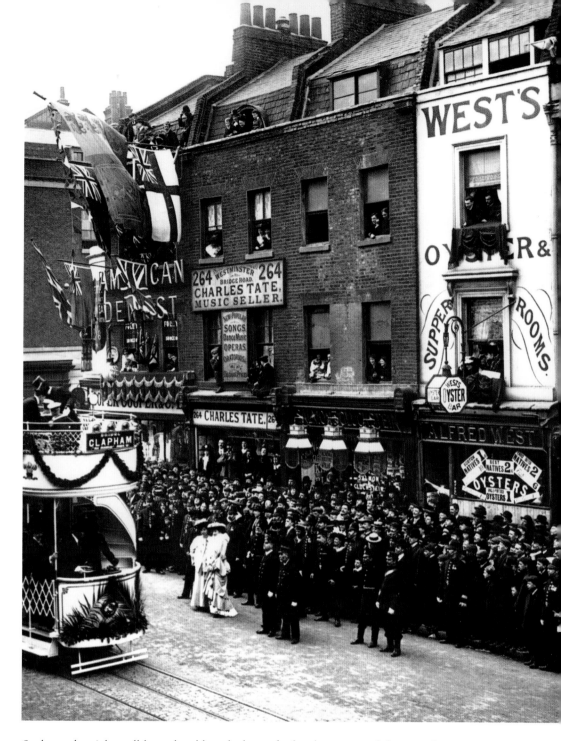

Such goods might well be ordered by telephone, for he also proposed the growth of telesales and mail-order shopping to stock 'the convenient home of the future, with its numerous electrical and mechanical appliances, and the various bicycles, motor-cars, photographic and phonographic apparatus that will be included in its equipment'. The house would probably be 'warmed in its walls from some power-generating station', or perhaps there would be a system by which 'air will enter the house of the future through proper tubes in the walls, which will warm it and capture its dust, and it will be spun out again through a simple mechanism'. He sketched the trend to en-suite conveniences by suggesting that 'every bedroom will have its own bath-dressing room' equipped with hot and cold water. As for cooking, the days of the cook 'working with a crimsoned face and bare, blackened arms' were numbered, for 'with a neat little range, heated by electricity and provided with thermometers, with absolutely controllable temperatures and proper heat screens, cooking might very easily be made a pleasant amusement.'

30   THE NORTHAMPTON INDEPENDENT.   December 19th, 1908.

ELECTRIC NOVELTIES make USEFUL PRESENTS.

Wells even predicted green roofs, still an aspiration for today's environmental movement: chimneys, he maintained, would disappear, making 'the roof a clean and pleasant addition to the garden spaces of the home'.

The people who would dominate this new world would, Wells thought, be educated middle-class professionals, engineers and scientists. These 'efficients' would be the driving force of his New Republic, gradually ousting the non-efficient rentiers, living off income from property or share dividends, whom he considered to be parasites on the society of his day. Nor would there be any place for the unskilled, uneducated masses, named by Wells the 'People of the Abyss'. Instead, an expanded and productive middle class would live in a globalised world in which formerly hostile nations might finally come together. Wells postulated that the 'splendid dream of a Federal Europe … may perhaps, after all, come to something like realisation at the opening of the 21st [century]', but he did not foresee a place within it for the United Kingdom; instead, Britain and the USA would gradually merge to form the core of an English-speaking bloc.

Fiction and fact

Inevitably, Wells got some things very wrong. Most notably, writing just two years before the Wright brothers' first flight, he vastly underestimated the future significance of air travel, stating that he did not 'think it at all probable that aeronautics will ever come into play as a serious modification of transport and communication'. More understandably, he failed to predict the internet, although perhaps he came as close as anyone could by foreseeing telegraph machinery 'in every post office and nearly every private house' carrying 'the latest stock prices, lottery draws and racing results'. Like all prophecies, Wells's work was very much a product of its day. For the Edwardian era was a time when thoughtful people of all persuasions sensed change in the air, even if few, if any, followed the idea through with anything approaching Wells's intellectual rigour. He was not alone in welcoming the breakdown of old rigidities and looking forward with excitement as well as concern to the new world that was dawning.

At the very time when Wells was making his predictions, scientists and engineers were at work helping to create the technological future of his imaginings. In the year that Wells was writing, the Italian-born Guglielmo Marconi sent the

TECHNOLOGICAL ADVANCES
For far-sighted observers the world in 1900 was already growing smaller. Trains and ocean-going liners had reduced travel times, and they would soon be shrunk further by the coming of aviation. Telephone exchanges like this one in Manchester were humming with activity, and providing new work opportunities for women. Radio would soon supply a medium for almost-instant delivery of messages; Marconi's first trans-Atlantic transmissions took place early in

the decade, bringing competition for the existing ocean-crossing telegraph cables. For the average householder, such developments were less significant at the time than devices that helped in the home. Gas lighting was widespread in cities by the turn of the century, and soon there was growing interest in electrical appliances like these ones advertised in a Northampton newspaper in 1908 (top left). Yet the market remained small; by 1910 just 2 per cent of British homes had electricity.

first wireless message across the Atlantic, from a transmission station in Ireland to a kite-supported antenna in St Johns, Newfoundland. In 1902 Oliver Heaviside proposed the existence of a layer of gas in what is now known as the ionosphere that would not allow electromagnetic waves to escape into space; it is this band, now known as the Heaviside Layer, that bounces radio signals back to Earth, making global broadcasting possible. Even more radically, the New Zealand-born physicist Ernest Rutherford was making fundamental discoveries about the nature of matter; revealed to the world in his 1904 book *Radioactivity*, these would pave the way for the splitting of the atom. The world was indeed changing, even if most people could only sense the coming transformations dimly.

EXPLORERS IN ANTARCTICA

The heroic age of Antarctic exploration got underway in 1897 with a Belgian expedition that unintentionally became the first to over-winter in the Antarctic Circle when its ship became icebound in the Bellingshausen Sea. The first British-financed expedition set out the following year; led by the Norwegian Carsten Borchgrevnik, it spent the winter on the Antarctic mainland at Cape Adare. In 1901 Captain Robert Falcon Scott (right) led a more ambitious venture; their equipment included a tethered observation balloon used for aerial surveys (left). Besides undertaking scientific work, Scott led a sledge team consisting of himself, Ernest Shackleton and Edward Wilson on a journey further south than anyone before them, coming within 500 miles of the Pole. The three-man team is pictured above celebrating Christmas 1902, shortly before returning to base camp. The other great Antarctic enterprise in the decade was the 1907-9 *Nimrod* expedition led by Shackleton (top left). Basing himself, like Scott before him, in McMurdo Sound, Shackleton took a different route to within 100 miles of the Pole before bad weather and the prospect of starvation forced him and his team to return to base. As the decade ended the Pole remained unconquered, but the Antarctic was firmly fixed in the public imagination as an arena that tested the limits of human endurance.

KEEPING
A STEADY
COURSE

By the summer of 1902 Lord Salisbury, 72 years old and in ailing health, was ready to step down from the premiership. He did not look far for a successor. Arthur Balfour, the rising star of the Conservative Party, was the obvious choice – he was also Salisbury's nephew.

STEADY AS SHE GOES Onlookers watch the launch of the battlecruiser HMS *Indomitable* from Glasgow docks in March 1907. Britain was still a world leader in shipbuilding at the time.

ARTFUL ARTHUR – THE NEW PM

Balfour owed his promotion to his uncle, Lord Salisbury, who had chosen him as his parliamentary private secretary in 1878 and then, in 1887, made him Chief Secretary for Ireland – a shock appointment said to have given rise to the expression 'Bob's your uncle!' (coined for Robert, Lord Salisbury). Balfour took a carrot-and-stick approach to Ireland. On the one hand he sought to subdue the desire for Home Rule by alleviating poverty and helping Irish tenants to buy the land they farmed. On the other, he sought to end nationalist protest by bringing in legislation to ban boycotts and intimidation; when police enforcing the new law killed three demonstrators, nationalists dubbed him 'bloody Balfour'.

At Westminster, his tenure as Irish secretary was generally considered a success, establishing his credentials as a potential Conservative leader. He enhanced his claim by his eloquence and subtlety as a parliamentary speaker. Nobody ever doubted his intelligence, least of all Balfour himself, who once said of a colleague 'If he had a little more brains he'd be a half-wit'. He was also perhaps the only British premier to write books on metaphysics, notably a *Defence of Philosophic Doubt* and a study of theology entitled *The Foundations of Belief*.

BACHELOR BALFOUR
Conservative Prime Minister Arthur Balfour had been born into the enchanted circle of well-connected families who dominated politics in late Victorian times. His mother was the daughter of the 2nd Marquess of Salisbury and his father was a millionaire Scottish landowner and MP. His father died when Arthur was just 8 years old, leaving him one of the wealthiest heirs in Britain. He studied at Eton and at Trinity College, Cambridge, and became an MP at the age of 26, with a seat in Cabinet before he was 40. One of the few major setbacks in his seemingly charmed life was the death from typhus of Mary Lyttelton, a cousin whom he had hoped to marry and the love of his life. Perhaps this sadness helps to explain why, for all his gifts, he remained an aloof figure who once declared: 'Nothing matters very much, and most things don't matter at all.' One of his few passions was golf; for a time he was captain of the Royal and Ancient Golf Club of St Andrews.

CHANGE IN THE CLASSROOM

By 1900 Britain had many more primary schools than three decades earlier, when the Education Act of 1870 had set out to promote state schooling. Yet politicians and employers alike felt that the nation was falling behind its Continental rivals, particularly Germany. Balfour described the system set up under the 1870 Act as 'chaotic, ineffectual, and utterly behind the age'. By its terms, the administration of the nation's schools was devolved to some 2,500 separate school boards. The vast majority of state-school pupils finished their education at age 12; barely 2 per cent went on to any kind of secondary study at all. As a result a new Education Bill was introduced which passed into law in 1902. This scrapped the school boards set up since 1870 and instead placed all state-funded schools under the control of newly established local education authorities, which were also given powers to vet teaching standards and promote secondary learning. The system brought in under the 1902 Act is the basis of state education in England and Wales to this day.

NON-CONFORMIST ANGER

Uncontroversial though it may now seem, Balfour's 1902 Education Act roused deep passions at the time. Most of the opposition came from Methodists and other Non-conformist religious groups who saw the measure as a surreptitious way of providing tax-financed subsidies for Church of England schools. A Baptist minister named John Clifford led the campaign, staging large-scale demonstrations like the march below on the Thames Embankment in London. The National Passive Resistance Committee led by Clifford encouraged supporters to refuse to pay the education rates, and over 170 people eventually went to prison for doing so. The bill itself went through 59 days of heated debate in Parliament before it was passed into law. Resentment of the Act soon melted away once its provisions came into effect.

In his term as Prime Minister, Balfour's main achievement was the Education Act of 1902, which laid the foundations of the modern state education system in England and Wales. The measure built on its 1870 predecessor, by which school boards had been set up in order to build schools and provide elementary education for children up to the age of 12. In practice, however, more children had continued to attend so-called 'voluntary' institutions, mostly run by the Church of England, than the new board schools. Balfour's bill sought to bring British practice into line with the best Continental models. It abolished the school boards and instead placed all schools, whether voluntary or state-supported, under local authority control. It also encouraged county councils to promote secondary education, with the result that the number of state-aided schools for teenagers doubled within five years of the Act coming into force.

Surprising as it may seem today, the Education Act proved controversial, mainly because it provided state funding for Church schools. Non-conformists railed against what they termed 'religion on the rates', seeing the grants as a surreptitious way of providing government financial support for the Anglican establishment. Yet the changes brought in by the Act quickly bedded down and were never subsequently challenged. In effect, Balfour's move provided a ladder

by which more able pupils from the lower-middle and working classes could pursue their studies beyond the age of 12. By 1910 there were over 150,000 students in state-supported secondary institutions.

Forging foreign alliances

The changes that took place in British foreign policy in the Balfour years had equal longterm significance. The main drift was away from Salisbury's position of 'splendid isolation' towards closer ties with selected overseas allies. Britain had been forced into cooperation with foreign powers in 1900, when the Boxer Rebellion erupted in China. Angered by the level of overseas involvement in China, and with the sanction of the dowager-empress Cixi, the Boxer rebels (the Chinese name translates as the 'Righteous and Harmonious Fists') attacked and killed Christian missionaries and Chinese Christians, and besieged the foreign legations in Beijing. The uprising was eventually put down by a multi-national force that brought together troops from eight countries, with Britain, Japan and Russia the biggest contributors. Cooperation with Japan was subsequently extended into a full-scale alliance, signed in London's Lansdowne House in 1902.

The Continental opposition to Britain's involvement in the Boer War had shown just how exposed the nation's position had become within Europe. Through the diplomacy of Otto von Bismarck, the German Chancellor, two blocs had formed in the previous decades, one linking Germany with Austro-Hungary and Italy, the other comprising France and Russia. For a time Salisbury and Balfour hesitated between the two: Germany was the rising power, but it also showed a competitive urge that made it a potential threat.

So Balfour was already inclining towards the notion of alliance with France when it was announced that Edward VII would visit Paris as part of a 1903 tour of European capitals. There was apprehension in advance of the visit and little warmth in the reception that the King received on first arrival. Then, on a visit to the theatre, Edward noticed a French actress in the foyer whom he had previously seen on the London stage. Abandoning protocol, he made his way over to kiss her hand, complimenting her on a performance that represented 'all the grace and spirit of France'. This exhibition of gallantry was widely reported in the press the following morning, triggering a burst of enthusiasm for the King. He was subsequently applauded on a visit to the Longchamp race-course and cheered on his way to a state banquet at the Elysée Palace.

By the end of Edward's visit, relations between the two nations were appreciably warmer, paving the way for the 1904 agreements known as the Entente Cordiale. This historic rapprochement established an Anglo-French alliance that would last through two world wars. It marked a joint awareness of the growing might of

MAKING FRIENDS
A French cartoon of President Emile Loubet and Edward VII, on the occasion of the King's visit to Paris in 1903, reflects the new spirit of political friendship between the two nations. Previously, relations had been distinctly frosty. Quite apart from the historical differences dividing them, conflicting colonial ambitions had brought Britain and France to the brink of war over the Fashoda crisis of 1899. There was also disagreement over the Boer War, for which Britain was widely condemned in France, as across most of mainland Europe. At the turn of the century tensions had been high enough to force Edward to abandon a trip to the Paris International Exhibition through fears for his safety. By 1903 both nations had reason to seek a *rapprochement*, stimulated in part by a fear of the growing might of Germany. Old rivalries were put aside and a new sense of amity prevailed.

Germany, as well as a desire to avoid colonial clashes of the type that had soured relations between the two powers in the closing decades of the 19th century.

The new mood of conciliation eventually extended to France's ally Russia, despite a bizarre and tragic incident in the Channel in October 1903. Having become embroiled with Japan in the Far East, the Tsar dispatched his Baltic fleet to sail halfway round the world to confront the enemy in the Pacific Ocean. The ships happened by night on a group of Hull trawlers fishing on the Dogger Bank. Mistaking them for Japanese torpedo boats, Russian warships opened fire, sinking one smack and killing two men (a third later died of wounds sustained in the attack). In the confusion, they also fired on one another, causing further casualties.

At a time of heightened tension, this tragic farce could have been the spark for war. But although there was much anger in Britain, the incident was settled through diplomatic channels. The Russian government agreed to pay £66,000 in compensation – a huge sum at the time – and the responsible officers were disciplined. A statue still stands in Hull commemorating the dead seamen. Anglo-Russian relations were not permanently damaged and within three years of the clash diplomats from both sides were signing an entente of their own, calming the fears of Russian encroachment on India that had for so long caused friction between the two great powers.

TURNING ON THE CHARM

Britain's closer ties with France were due in no small part to the influence of the King himself. A keen Francophile, Edward enjoyed a holiday every year at Biarritz on the Bay of Biscay. His 1903 visit to the French capital turned into an extraordinary personal triumph. On his way from a state banquet at the Elysée Palace to the British Embassy he was mobbed by French crowds shouting 'Vive Edouard!'. He is seen here acknowledging the crowd at Longchamp, the famous French racecourse in the Bois de Boulogne, where a one-day meeting was specially arranged in his honour, with every race named after horses that had belonged to the King.

DIVISIONS OVER EMPIRE

In the wider world beyond Europe, policy continued to be dominated by imperial matters. By 1900 the British Empire was, in geographical terms, nearing its greatest extent. The new decade saw further expansion. On 1 January, 1900, the government took over lands in West Africa that had been administered privately by the Royal Niger Company; these were combined with the small Niger Coast Protectorate to form the colony of Southern Nigeria. In the same year an amorphous protectorate was proclaimed over Northern Nigeria; military action was subsequently required to extend British control over the emirate of Kano.

Incursion into Tibet

Lord Curzon, the autocratic Viceroy of India, launched an altogether more ambitious venture when he dispatched a force several thousand strong under Major Francis Younghusband into the mountains of Tibet. Younghusband set out in the hope of negotiating a trade agreement and countering Russian influence, always feared as a potential threat on the northern borders of the Raj. When the Dalai Lama refused to respond, Curzon sent more troops, many of them Gurkhas and Pathan hill people from the other side of the border, with instructions to march on Lhasa, a forbidden city then virtually unknown in the West.

The Tibetans chose to resist, and an extraordinary campaign ensued as the imperial force pressed forward through some of the world's most difficult terrain.

REMOTE RULER
At the time of the British military incursion, Tibet was in effect ruled by Thubten Gyatso, the 13th Dalai Lama (right). It was largely Thubten's friendship with Agvan Drozhiev, a Mongolian Buddhist monk who had served as his tutor and who happened to be a Russian citizen, that persuaded the British authorities in India that Russia had designs on the country. On receiving news of the invasion, Thubten took Drozhiev's advice to flee to Mongolia, 1500 miles away. In his absence the Chinese, who already claimed suzerainty over Tibet, sought to reassert their sovereignty, but were unable to enforce their rule. Thubten eventually returned to Tibet late in 1908, only to be forced out again less than two years later, this time by a Chinese invasion. By then Britain had settled its differences with Russia in the Anglo–Russian Entente of 1907, making the reasons for the 1904 incursion into Tibet less relevant than ever.

FACES OF EMPIRE
'My name is George Nathaniel Curzon,
I am a most superior person …' So began a
famous rhyme describing Baron Curzon of
Kedleston (left), Viceroy of India from 1899
to 1905. Highly educated and much
travelled, the aristocratic statesman
became obsessed with the danger that
Russian territorial ambitions were thought
to present to the northern frontier of the
British Raj. Responding to rumours that
Russian influence was on the rise in Lhasa,
the Tibetan capital, he determined in 1903
to counter it by force. He despatched a
military expedition to Tibet under the
command of Francis Younghusband
(above), a career military officer who
shared Curzon's own passion for
adventurous journeys in little-known
regions. Younghusband's incursion was met
by fierce resistance, but the British imperial
troops reached the Tibetan capital in
August 1904. Yet the achievement brought
no political gains and proved expensive in
cash and lives, particularly Tibetan ones.

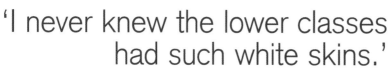

'I never knew the lower classes
had such white skins.'

Lord Curzon, on seeing soldiers bathing

The defenders fought bravely, but had no answer to British Maxim guns; several thousand Tibetans died while inflicting a couple of hundred fatalities on the invaders. Younghusband eventually reached his destination in August 1904, eight months after setting out from base camp, only to find that the Dalai Lama had fled to Outer Mongolia. Younghusband imposed a punitive settlement on the Dalai Lama's deputy, which was never in fact fully implemented, then withdrew to India. The incursion, although a remarkable feat of arms, achieved little except to further humiliate China, which had proved incapable of defending the Tibetan territory that nominally came under its protective aegis.

Anti-imperialist views

The Tibetan expedition proved controversial back in London, where the appetite for colonial adventure was much reduced in the wake of the Boer War. A current of liberal opinion now viewed all such enterprises as greedy and unproductive. In 1902, J A Hobson had published *Imperialism*, a highly influential book in which he argued that the scramble for colonies in the late 19th century had not been driven by any real national interest but rather by international financiers interested in quick profits. Such views lay behind a fierce wave of agitation that opposed Balfour's decision, in the wake of the Boer War, to allow indentured Chinese labour into South Africa to work the Witwatersrand gold mines.

The natural home of such hostility to unbridled imperialism was the Liberal Party, and as long as the Conservatives remained in power, the imperial cause was firmly in the ascendant. Its greatest champion was Joseph Chamberlain, Unionist *par excellence*, who would declare, in a 1906 speech, 'England without an empire! Can you conceive it? England in that case would not be the England we love.'

> 'A nation may … like Great Britain, neglect its agriculture, and fall behind other nations in its methods of education in order that it may squander its resources in finding speculative fields of investment in distant corners of the Earth …'
>
> J A Hobson, in *Imperialism*

Chamberlain's 'imperial preference'

Yet Chamberlain's very enthusiasm for the imperial cause would itself become deeply divisive in the Conservative Party. Ever since the repeal of the Corn Laws in 1846, Victorian Britain had remained wedded to the cause of free trade. For much of that time the nation had prospered, but by 1900 British merchants were feeling the pinch of competition from overseas, with the greatest challenge coming from the rising economies of Germany and the USA. In these circumstances Chamberlain thought he saw an opportunity to boost the Empire at the same time as bolstering Conservative support among the business community and generating government revenue for social welfare initiatives to boot. Promoting what he viewed as a win-win solution, he proposed a system of customs tariffs on goods imported from countries beyond the Empire's bounds.

As opponents both within and outside the Conservative Party were quick to point out, there were disadvantages to his strategy of Imperial Preference, as it

became known. On the one hand it would inevitably encourage the erection of similar trade barriers against British goods in the countries to which it applied; on the other, it would increase the cost of imports from lands outside the Empire, and these included some of Britain's major trading partners. In particular, the nation brought in huge amounts of wheat from the USA, as well as beef from Argentina and dairy products from Denmark and the Netherlands. The inevitable result would be a substantial hike in the cost of food.

In the years between 1903 and 1905 the Conservatives split down the middle over the issue of preferential tariffs. In its way, Imperial Preference was as divisive for the party as the question of relations with the European Community would be in the 1990s. Free-traders, including Balfour's Chancellor of the Exchequer, C T Ritchie, passionately opposed the policy. Finding his plans stymied by such opposition, Chamberlain announced his intention to resign from the Cabinet.

Balfour had refused to commit himself to either side in the argument, seeking to straddle the growing divide. Now, he accepted Chamberlain's decision to resign, but sought to balance it by also forcing the resignation from the Cabinet of Ritchie and another prominent free-trader, Lord Balfour of Burleigh, the Secretary for Scotland. Other demissions followed, and in 1904 a rising young Conservative MP, just 29 years old and recently back from adventures in the Boer War, crossed the floor to join the Liberal Party over the issue. His name was Winston Churchill.

Balfour's bane

The split that was tearing the Unionists apart failed to bring out the best in their Prime Minister. Balfour was often accused of viewing the world with lofty intellectual detachment – as the Socialist leader Ramsey Macdonald would one day put it, 'He saw a great deal of life from afar'. In this moment of crisis his instinct was to look for a middle way between free trade and protectionism. He proposed a policy of retaliatory tariffs that would only apply to nations that themselves placed duties on British imports. The result was an unsatisfactory compromise that pleased neither side of the party.

Meanwhile, Chamberlain was using his new-found freedom from the restraints of Cabinet membership to carry the crusade for Imperial Preference across the country. Adopting the slogan 'Tariff Reform Means Work for All!', he attracted vast crowds with his passionate oratory. Soon a newly formed Tariff Reform League was expensively touting the virtues of his plan, and something like open

continued on page 65

POPULAR PREFERENCE
Seen here being greeted by supporters in the run-up to the 1906 general election, Joseph Chamberlain made himself the spokesman for Imperial Preference – a policy of creating preferential trade tariffs for empire-made goods. The scheme, seen by its opponents as a protectionist attack on free trade, split the Conservative Party, contributing more than any other factor to the Liberal victory. It was the second time that Chamberlain had caused such a rift; 20 years earlier he had left the Liberals over the issue of Irish Home Rule, taking a considerable section of the party with him.

A WORLDWIDE WEB OF TRADE

Seaborne trade, like the goods seen here piled up in Liverpool docks, was the lifeblood of Edwardian Britain – literally so, as the nation had come to rely on food imports to keep the population from going hungry. Even the production of staples like Cadbury's cocoa (below) presupposed regular deliveries of raw beans from colonies in Africa. There were worries, though, that Britain's international position in terms of both trade and manufacturing was deteriorating; while manufacturing exports increased by 30 per cent between 1885 and 1900, those for Germany grew twice as fast over the same period and the value of US exports almost doubled. The discontent of manufacturers about competition from foreign produce was one of the main forces that drove the protectionist campaign for Imperial Preference, begun by Joseph Chamberlain. Ultimately, the campaign was divisive and led to a humiliating defeat for the Conservatives at the general election of January 1906. The Liberal Party were returned to power on a policy of continued free trade.

YOUNG WINSTON
Winston Churchill was 30 years old when this portrait was taken in 1904, and he had already packed more adventure into his first three decades than most politicians see in a lifetime. Born at Blenheim Palace, the eldest son of the Conservative MP Lord Randolph Churchill, he at first pursued a military career, seeing active service in Malakand (in what is now Pakistan) and in the Sudan, where he participated in a cavalry charge at the Battle of Omdurman. Covering the Boer War as a newspaper correspondent, he was captured and subsequently escaped from a prisoner-of-war camp, trekking almost 300 miles to safety through hostile territory. Elected a Conservative MP in the Khaki Election of 1900, he later crossed the House to the Liberals over the issue of Imperial Preference, which he opposed.

warfare had broken out between protectionists and free traders within the Unionist ranks. Balfour's authority was fatally weakened.

In this extremity the Prime Minister made a fateful decision. Hoping that the Liberals, who had divisions of their own, might be unable to form a functioning government, he resigned office in December 1905. But the prospect of power concentrated Liberal minds wonderfully. Before the year was out their leader Henry Campbell-Bannerman was ensconced as Prime Minister in Balfour's place, at the head of a Cabinet firmly committed to free trade.

In the general election that followed, in January 1906, the Conservatives and Unionists were routed, losing more than half their seats and putting an end to two decades of predominantly Tory rule. The Liberals returned to power with 397 out of the 670 available seats, the greatest electoral victory in their history. In the general rout even Balfour lost his seat in Manchester East; he rapidly returned to the House via a safe seat in the City of London, but no-one doubted the depth of the humiliation he had suffered.

PRESS BARONS AND MUSIC-HALL DUCHESSES

One reason why Imperial Preference achieved such traction was the noisy backing it received from much of the British press. The development of mass-market journalism catering for the newly literate class emerging from the board schools had been one of the most significant innovations of the past two decades. The pioneer of the movement was the publisher George Newnes whose weekly *Tit-Bits*, presenting itself as a digest of the most interesting news snippets from all the world's periodicals, built up a circulation of over half a million readers.

One man to see the possibilities was Alfred Harmsworth. By the age of 23 he had launched a rival to *Tit-Bits* called *Answers to Correspondents*. The publication thrived on promotions, which Harmsworth did much to pioneer, including one promising 'a pound a week for life' – the answer given by a tramp on the Embankment when the budding publishing mogul asked him what he most dreamed of possessing. Other weeklies followed, and they were successful enough to encourage Harmsworth to move into daily newspapers. Starting with the *London Evening News*, which he bought in 1894, he went on to found the *Daily Mail* two years later. Right from the start the *Mail* threw itself behind the Unionist cause; its hero was Joseph Chamberlain, its villains anyone perceived to stand in the way of Empire, a notable target being Emily Hobhouse who campaigned against the treatment of civilian prisoners in concentration camps in the Boer War.

Soon Harmsworth himself was successful enough in the newspaper business to attract competitors. Another entrepreneur, Arthur Pearson, established the *Daily Express* in 1900 to compete with the *Mail*. A clergyman's son educated at

Winchester School, Pearson introduced the innovation – radical at the time – of putting news on the paper's front page, rather than advertisements.

Harmsworth responded in 1903 with the *Daily Mirror*, originally targeted at a female audience and boasting 'an all woman staff for an all woman readership'. When that experiment failed, he relaunched the paper with a male editor, a reduced cover price, and a new, tabloid format, stipulating that no story should run to over 250 words. Other elements of Harmsworth's formula for the *Mirror* included the use of subheads to break up lengthy columns of text, the substitution of photographs for old-fashioned line drawings, and the introduction of gossip columns, household hints, competitions and special offers.

For his services to the media, Harmsworth was made 1st Viscount Northcliffe in Balfour's dissolution Honours List in 1905. He had earlier joked 'When I want a peerage I will pay for it like an honest man', and he did in fact receive it after investing large amounts of money in a local newspaper in Manchester, where Balfour had his seat, promising to make it 'the leading Conservative organ of the North'. In the years that followed he moved into quality journalism, buying up *The Observer* and then *The Times*. At first he struggled to raise the circulation of that ailing colossus, but eventually quadrupled its readership, primarily by the expedient of reducing the cover price to 1 penny.

Throughout the decade Harmsworth was a noisy, energetic presence who did much to liven up the press of the day. He had few doubts of his own importance, yet the extent of the political influence of his publications is uncertain. Few of the causes that he campaigned for – whether to boost British aviation, or to persuade

PIONEERS OF MASS JOURNALISM
Almost exact contemporaries, being born and dying within a year of one another, Alfred Harmsworth (above left) and Arthur Pearson (above) between them did much to create mass-market journalism in Britain. Harmsworth, later ennobled as Lord Northcliffe, founded the *Daily Mail* and *Daily Mirror*. Pearson created the *Daily Express* and also at one time ran the *Evening Standard*. In other respects, their lives were very different. Pearson was educated at Winchester and generally had an easier childhood than Northcliffe, who was the son of an alcoholic barrister. In later life, Pearson was progressively blinded by glaucoma, eventually losing his sight altogether. Northcliffe ruffled many feathers during his career – Lloyd George once said of him 'Even the Almighty formed a Trinity. Northcliffe is a Unitarian.' Yet this did not stop the politician making use of the press baron's talents – Harmsworth served as director of propaganda in Lloyd George's war-time cabinet.

VOICE OF THE PEOPLE

Born Tilly Wood, the singer who became famous as Marie Lloyd was the eldest of 12 children. Her parents lived in the Hoxton district of inner-city London, earning their living by making artificial flowers on piecework for an Italian dealer. Encouraged by an aunt who was a dancer, Marie began performing in public from the age of 5 and started her professional career aged just 15. Within a year, she was earning up to £100 a week in the big West End music halls, and she remained a star until her death 37 years later. In the so-called 'Music-Hall War' of 1907, when music hall performers went on strike for better pay and conditions, Lloyd came out in support of the strikers, stating 'We [the stars] are fighting not for ourselves but for the poorer members of the profession, earning 30 shillings to £3 a week'. The strike ended in arbitration, with the performers winning a minimum-wage agreement.

readers of the benefits of wholemeal bread – had much success, and the Liberal landslide of 1906 was won despite the hostility of all the Northcliffe newspapers.

Music to remember

The Edwardian age saw the last great flowering of music hall, with stars like George Robey, Harry Lauder, Vesta Tilley, Harry Champion, Little Tich and above all the great Marie Lloyd, all in their prime. In an age without radio, television, cinema or the internet, the demand for live entertainment was huge, and the music halls set out to fill it. In 1900 there were around 50 of them in the Greater London region alone and well over 200 in the rest of the country, with half a dozen each in Birmingham, Glasgow and Liverpool. Once raucous, music halls had become far more respectable since the 1880s, when legislation confined the sale of alcohol to licensed bars behind the stalls and circle. The subsequent reduction in drunkenness had turned them more into centres of family entertainment.

A typical variety bill included a dozen or so short acts, so stars moved from venue to venue, appearing in as many as four theatres in a single night. Alongside singers and stand-up comics there might be acrobats and dancers, notably the Tiller Girls, whose high-kicking, linked-arm precision routines were learned in a special school set up by the entrepreneur John Tiller. Even hard-up customers

continued on page 75

A NIGHT OF VARIETY

Music halls were at their peak as the 20th century dawned. Their origins in public-house 'singing rooms' had been left far behind – especially since alcohol consumption had been restricted to the theatre bars – and the halls had found their role in providing good variety entertainment. The core audience was drawn from lower-middle and working-class families, who now had more cash and leisure time than in the past. And as most of the performers shared the same background, attitudes and values, there was a real sense of community between stage and stalls.

MUSIC HALLS TO MUSICALS

In the days before cinema and television, live light entertainment was thriving in theatres and halls up and down the country. Music hall reigned supreme, but other forms of stage entertainment were also popular, in particular the musical comedy. The three ladies on the right were part of the chorus in 'The Dairymaids', a musical farce staged at London's Apollo in 1906. The show was successful enough to go to New York for a season the next year, then return for a revival in London in 1908.

The music hall stars were household names and easily crossed over into other shows, especially pantomime – like northeast England's Bessie Featherstone (left). In fact, the combination of humour and musical talent made music·hall performers the stalwarts of pantomime, that peculiarly British phenomenon of the winter season on stage.

GLAMOUR AND GAIETY
Talented, attractive female stars like the princely costumed – and tiny-waisted – Vesta Tilley (left) were intrinsic to the appeal of music hall. But although the halls were in their prime throughout the Edwardian years, some signs of their future decline were already becoming apparent. One was the coming of moving pictures. By the latter part of the decade many variety bills included a feature called the Bioscope – a few minutes of grainy, silent, black-and-white film projected onto a big screen to a musical accompaniment.

The other new rival, rather closer in spirit to the fare on offer in the music halls themselves, was the musical comedy – a 20th-century updating of the operettas of Victorian times, as well as of Gilbert and Sullivan's hugely popular comic operas. The pioneer of the new style was an impresario named George Edwardes who, having worked with Gilbert and Sullivan, had come to realise that there was also a market for less intellectual, more family-friendly fare. His Gaiety Theatre in London – rebuilt as the New Gaiety in 1903 – was the showcase for the new form. The Gaiety Girls who performed there became the pin-ups of Edwardian London, attracting 'stage-door Johnnies', so called because they lingered outside the theatre hoping to take a girl to dinner. Edwardes' greatest hit was with Franz Lehar's *The Merry Widow*, which was staged not at the Gaiety but at Daly's Theatre in Leicester Square. Starring Lily Elsie in the title role (right), it became one of the greatest hits of the decade, running for 778 performances; Edward VII saw it four times.

PALACES OF MIRTH
As the name on the posters suggests (left), the grander music halls set out to conjure an air of opulence that set them apart from the surrounding urban drabness. In contrast, the artists who played there kept their material as close as possible to everyday life. George Robey (above) was unusual in coming from a middle-class background; his father was an engineer, and Robey himself briefly attended Cambridge University. On stage, he was billed as the 'Prime Minister of Mirth' and specialised in deflationary humour. He often performed in drag and pioneered some familiar camp mannerisms, such as telling a laughing audience to 'Desist!' – a trick picked up later by Frankie Howerd.

RAISING A LAUGH

The soul of the music hall lay in the performers, particularly the comedians. Little Tich (left), just 4ft 6in tall, was one of the best-loved of all. He was famous for his 'Big Boot' routine wearing extra long shoes; his dexterity might have been helped by the curious fact that he had six digits on each hand and foot. The career of singer-comic Harry Lauder (top left) took a major leap forward in 1900 when he first performed in music hall in London. He became a huge international star, as popular in America and Australia as he was at home. The trio above were comic stalwarts of Drury Lane pantomimes: from bottom to top, Herbert Campbell, Johnny Danvers and the great Dan Leno.

FOREVER YOUNG

Peter Pan, the timeless creation of J M Barrie, made his debut on the London stage on 27 December, 1904. The character had already appeared in Barrie's novel *The Little White Bird*, published two years earlier; following the play's success, the section of the book featuring Peter was published separately as a children's book under the title *Peter Pan in Kensington Gardens*. The convention of Peter being played by a young woman, as in the tradition of pantomime principal boys – this photograph shows Stephanie Stephens in the Peter Pan role – dates back to the very first performance. It got around the practical difficulty of finding young male actors suitable for the part, particularly as the children of the Darling family, whom Peter befriends in the play, had to be even younger. More than a century later, Barrie's story has lost none of its charm.

SUPERSLEUTH

The American actor-manager William Gillette strikes a familiar pose as Arthur Conan Doyle's celebrated detective in a 1901 stage production of *Sherlock Holmes*. Conan Doyle had first introduced Holmes 14 years earlier in the novel *A Study in Scarlet*, and the character had proved an instant success, but he had trouble adapting the stories for the stage. Eventually, he ended up co-authoring the play with William Gillette, who also took the title role. The production was a great success, and Gillette went on to give more than 1,300 performances as Holmes across the USA and Britain.

could afford a few pence for a seat in the gallery, where they sat crammed onto benches without back supports – as one audience member later recalled, 'you often got someone's feet in your back or orange peel down your neck'.

The plus side of the enforced intimacy in the audience was a wonderful sense of community that seasoned performers used to their advantage. Harry Lauder's winning combination of Lowland Scots wit and sentimental balladry would eventually make him the first British artist to sell more than a million records. Yet no-one worked the halls more effectively than Marie Lloyd, who attracted admirers from all backgrounds. The poet T S Eliot wrote of her 'genius' and her 'capacity for expressing the soul of the people'. To her core working-class audience, Marie was family. They loved her for the sentiment of her songs, for her Cockney humour and mildly risqué double-entendres, and for never forgetting where she came from. She retained her popularity to the end; when she died in 1922, more than 100,000 people paid their respects at her funeral procession.

Signs of change – moving pictures

Significantly for the future, moving pictures were just beginning to establish a foothold. The very first public film show in Britain had taken place at the Regent Street Polytechnic in London in 1896, and moving pictures were still a novelty in the early 1900s. Entrepreneurs with projectors toured small towns, putting on shows in improvised venues. The first purpose-built picture house was opened in Colne, Lancashire, in 1907 by a former magic-lantern showman. By the following year the new art form was generating enough excitement to cause tragedy, when 16 children were crushed to death as a crowd of 400 fought to enter a 'moving-picture show' held in a rented church hall in Barnsley.

J B Priestley would later describe a visit to one of the early cinemas – 'a certain Theatre-de-Luxe, where for sixpence you were given an hour or so of short films, a cup of tea and a biscuit'. He was unimpressed by the experience, comparing it unfavourably (as did T S Eliot) with the camaraderie of the music hall. Yet the future would belong to the flickering images on the silver screen.

THE GAP BETWEEN RICH AND POOR

The Conservative electoral debacle of January 1906 represented something of a watershed in the Edwardian era. In retrospect, the years of Tory rule under Lord Salisbury and Balfour can be seen politically as a continuation of the late Victorian consensus. The mood was to change after the Liberal landslide, when a fresh awareness of the great divide that split British society came to the fore. In a time of general prosperity, observant citizens were more conscious than ever before of the yawning gap that separated the rich from the poor.

For the wealthiest section of society the decade was a time of conspicuous consumption, a term coined by the sociologist Thorstein Veblen in 1899 to describe the behaviour of America's new rich. Taxation was far less of a burden than it was to become: income tax was levied at just 5 per cent and only on incomes above £160 a year. Fewer than a million out of the 33 million residents of England and Wales paid any at all, while some 400,000 people declared incomes of over £400 – sufficient to support a comfortably upper-middle-class lifestyle.

In Britain, the tone was set by royalty itself, for in contrast to Victoria's style of relatively modest respectability, Edward radiated an appetite for lavish enjoyment. At the top of the wealth pyramid came the elite who made up 'society', described by the Liberal C F G Masterman, a critic, as 'an aggregation of clever, agreeable, often lovable people, whose material wants are satisfied by the labour of unknown workers in all the world, trying with a desperate seriousness to make something of a life spared the effort of wage-earning'.

The summer season

One focus for such efforts was the London season, which ran from the end of April to late July. Among its chief purposes was the finding of suitable husbands for eligible daughters, and a dizzying round of social occasions was provided for that purpose. One socialite recalled 'There were a minimum of four balls every night – six balls possibly', all duly listed in *The Times*. It was also *de rigueur* for debutantes to be presented at court at glamorous evening ceremonies.

continued on page 81

EN ROUTE TO THE REGATTA
Ladies dressed in elegant summer finery and gentlemen in blazers and boaters make their way along the platform at Henley railway station, en route for the annual rowing regatta. Held over the first weekend in July, the event was a fixture of the summer season. Competitors as well as spectators belonged to 'polite' society – the rules specifically excluded 'mechanics, artisans or labourers' from participating, along with anyone 'who engaged in any menial activity'. The prohibition against the working classes was only dropped in 1937.

COUNTRY PASSIONS

Hunting and shooting was a central part of the lifestyle of many landowning families in Edwardian times. The shooting season began in early August in time for the so-called 'Glorious Twelfth' – the 12th day of the month when the moorland grouse-shooting season opened. In lowland areas, the birds most often on the wrong end of a gun were pheasant and partridge, which like grouse had an open and close season. Keen shots like the country gent below could keep their eye in by targeting rabbits at any time of year; it helped to keep the rabbit numbers down and they all ended up in the pot. The fox-hunting fraternity observed strict social rituals that dictated even the number of buttons on riders' coats; the Master of the Hunt had four, huntsmen five. Cubbing – the practice of pursuing immature foxes with young hounds – usually began in autumn, shortly after the grouse season got under way.

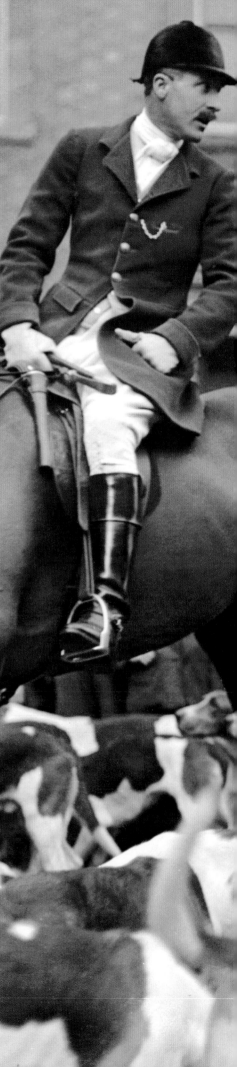

DRESSING FOR DINNER
For the well-to-do the formal dinner was a much-prized Edwardian institution. In society circles, according to Sir Charles Petrie, 'private dinner parties of 18 or 20 people were the rule rather than the exception, and the small dinner was unknown'. Hostesses were only able to contemplate such events thanks to the ready availability of servants to prepare and serve the food. For the most part, male guests still wore tailcoats; dinner jackets, known contemptuously as 'bum-freezers', were considered daringly modern. This group, photographed in 1909, were about to dine before attending a masonic ball.

For the older generation the season meant a round of parties rubbing shoulders with a familiar circle of friends and acquaintances, varied by visits to the opera, theatre and events such as the Royal Academy Summer Exhibition. There were sporting occasions like the Oxford-Cambridge Boat Race and the Eton-Harrow cricket match at Lord's, and excursions to Ascot or Goodwood for the racing. Husbands might seek sanctuary from domestic bliss in the gentlemen's clubs of Pall Mall, while a growing number of wives attended all-female establishments. There was horseriding along Rotten Row in Hyde Park, where the riders could see their peers and be seen by them, and might also catch a glimpse of the celebrated team of zebras that drew the carriage of the financier Leopold de Rothschild.

There was time, too, for shopping. By the 1900s the big department stores were coming into their own. Harrods, Whiteleys, Barkers of Kensington, Peter Jones and John Lewis were joined in 1909 by Selfridges, established at the unfashionable end of Oxford Street by the American entrepreneur Gordon Selfridge. The fashion-conscious made trips to Paris to buy designs by Doucet, Paquin and Worth. Life *à la mode* required a considerable amount of time to be spent on dressing. Ladies of the *beau monde* might change their outfit three times or more in a day: a tailored costume was worn for morning calls and shopping, a looser tea gown could be worn for informal afternoon entertaining, then a spectacular silk or satin evening dress for the ball or theatre, worn with jewellery and perhaps a tiara.

Country living

When the season was over, society dispersed to country houses scattered across the land. For the men one of the main attractions was the shooting, and animal life was slaughtered on an industrial scale. Lord Ripon, a champion shot, accounted for over half a million head of game in his lifetime, all carefully annotated in his game books. Victor Cavendish, a Liberal Unionist MP and (as the Duke of Devonshire) a future Colonial Secretary, recorded a bag of 9,000 birds from a week's entertaining at Bolton Abbey.

Another major preoccupation was food – the Edwardian age was notable for the gargantuan appetites of the rich. Breakfast in the country might feature a choice of poached or scrambled eggs, bacon, ham, sausages, devilled kidneys and haddock, displayed on salvers and kept warm by spirit lamps. Then there would be cold meats, ranging from pressed beef and tongue to roast pheasant and grouse,

plus the usual range of porridge, scones, toast, marmalade and fruit. Evening meals could run in exceptional circumstances to as many as 12 courses. One formal dinner in London, given by the Conservative 1900 Club for colonial premiers, catered for 1,600 diners with, among other delicacies, 200 whole salmon, 2,500 quails, 25,000 asparagus sticks, 1,400 bottles of champagne and 300 bottles each of whisky, Chartreuse and brandy. Unsurprisingly in view of such indulgence, the Edwardian era also saw a fashion for taking the waters at health spas; Edward VII's favourite, Marienbad, was only one of many Continental locations favoured by the gentry.

A world apart

Needless to say, the world the poor inhabited was separated from the graciousness of country-house living by much more than the long drives and high walls that hid the great estates. Although this world, too, had its areas of privacy, it was in general more studied and observed than ever before, and the result was a growing awareness of poverty as a social problem that needed to be addressed.

Charles Booth had begun a pioneering study of the working classes in London in the late 1880s; it was published over the years in 17 volumes, the last of which appeared in 1903. Meanwhile Seebohm Rowntree, a scion of the Quaker chocolate dynasty, had been conducting a detailed survey of deprived families in York, which was published in 1901. Rowntree defined a living wage as being 7 shillings (35p) a week for a single man, or 21 shillings 8d (£1.08p) for a family of five. According to his observations, between a quarter and a third of the population of the city fell

MEAN STREETS
Life for poor working families, like this one photographed in their home in about 1900, was difficult at best. Long hours and low wages combined with bad living conditions to make sickness almost endemic. Poor housing with inadequate services was a persistent problem – in Birmingham, for example, there were areas where 30 people shared a single tap. In the most deprived parts of the cities renting rooms jointly and bed-sharing were not unknown; three people might rent the same bed in eight-hour shifts. Manual workers struggled to earn enough to support their families; ironically, the poor generally had more children than the rich – mining families, for example, averaged more than seven children compared to three or four in an upper-middle class family. The result was chronic malnutrition among the poor, only marginally eased by charitable hand-outs. These women and children with jugs (right) were queuing outside a soup-kitchen in Bury, Lancashire.

below this 'poverty line'. A similar conclusion was reached by the curiously titled Inter-Departmental Committee on Physical Deterioration, set up by Parliament in the wake of the Boer War; in 1904 it reported that a third of British schoolchildren regularly went hungry. Such studies revealed that poor families were in general larger than middle-class ones and many lived in unhealthily cramped conditions. Overcrowding was particularly bad in the city slums; the proportion of people living two or more to a room rose from a national average of 8.6 per cent to over 30 per cent in the East End and 59 per cent in parts of Glasgow.

In marked contrast to the feasts of the rich, the poor relied on bread as their staple. In an age before domestic gas or electricity was widely available, cooking was time-consuming and expensive, so a slice spread with a scraping of butter, lard or beef dripping, or perhaps with jam or a wedge of cheese, served regularly as a meal. Even so, most households except the very poorest would manage to afford a joint, usually of beef, for Sunday dinner. Contrary to popular prejudice – it was a widely held belief among the comfortable classes, for example, that if the workers were given baths, they would only use them for storing coal – hard-up families were often thrifty. A researcher in Lambeth discovered that most households there saved between 2.5 and 10 per cent of their income in funds designed to cover funeral expenses for family members.

continued on page 86

UNWANTED LEISURE TIME

In the days before state welfare, people lived in fear of unemployment, which could rapidly reduce them to penury. The first recourse of the jobless was usually help from relatives. After that they might turn to money-lenders; a survey in 1906 revealed 692 pawnshops within a 10-mile radius of the City of London.

There was little for working men to do in between looking for jobs except to kill time – in the parks if the weather was fine. This scene was photographed in London's St James's Park in the early 1900s. Policy-makers were acutely aware of the problem, and unemployment was a hot political issue of the day. Arthur Balfour's Conservative government introduced the Unemployed Workmen's Act in 1903 to establish local registers of the jobless, and in 1909 Winston Churchill, as President of the Board of Trade, created labour exchanges to help the unemployed to find new jobs.

STREET URCHINS
Barefoot children, like these young mites outside their slum-terrace home, were a common sight in city streets. As a result of overcrowding and malnutrition, many were in poor health; rickets, consumption, diphtheria and whooping cough all took a heavy toll on the young. Surveys showed that a third of state-school pupils regularly went hungry. The Liberal government sought to address the problem by passing the Provision of Meals Act in 1906, which permitted local authorities to provide subsidised food. Compulsory medical inspections in schools were introduced a year later, although treatment for the sick was not provided until 1912.

The cost of a burial might be manageable and planned for, but there was little that even the most prudent could do in the face of prolonged sickness or accident. At a time of minimal health and safety regulation injury at work was common and disasters causing fatalities occurred all too frequently: an explosion in 1909 at the Burns Pit in West Stanley, Co Durham, killed 168 people. Those who suffered lesser injuries often opted to look after themselves, for doctors' visits were expensive. If a doctor was called, he would sometimes do minor operations *in situ*, setting broken arms or legs on the kitchen table.

The 'people of the abyss'

For those who could not find work, the usual option was the workhouse. Conditions there were deliberately grim to discourage people from choosing to live on the public purse. Not surprisingly, some preferred to trust themselves to the streets; in London alone there were an estimated 35,000 vagrants in Edwardian times. There, too, the authorities made life as difficult as possible, closing the parks at night to ensure that the homeless had to keep moving or risk arrest. H G Wells called those trapped in the lower depths of society the 'People of the Abyss', and he was not alone. As awareness of the plight of the unemployed and poor spread, reformers reached out to help, demanding basic social welfare measures such as pensions and national insurance. In the wake of the Liberal electoral victory of 1906, such calls became too loud to ignore.

LAST STOP: THE WORKHOUSE

For people with no jobs and no money, the only choice was begging or the workhouse, known familiarly at the time as 'the spike'. Conditions inside were deliberately grim to deter the poor from entering and thus living at the expense of rate-payers. Inmates had to take a cold bath on arrival, and families were split up – mothers often only saw their children once a week. Able-bodied inmates were given work to do – for the women that often meant the workhouse's washing (above). Hygiene was generally poor: a survey in 1909 found 56 girls sharing a single tub of water and half a dozen towels; another institution had two small basins for 120 inmates and the toilets were locked at night. Food was not tempting, but for many it was no worse than the fare outside. Portions were weighed out by a warder – typically 6oz (170g) of bread a day with ¾ pint (400ml) of a porridge called skilly.

TIME FOR CHANGE

Some general elections merely confirm a party's hold on the country, or switch power between rival groups with broadly similar views. Others – like Attlee's Labour victory in 1945 or Thatcher's Conservative triumph of 1979 – mark a decisive shift in the nation's political orientation. The Liberal election victory of January 1906 was just such an election, bringing an end to two decades of Conservative rule and putting Britain in the hands of reformers with a thirst for radical change.

UP AND AWAY Intrepid balloonists rise above a crowd of well-dressed onlookers at the Hurlingham Club in Fulham, London, in 1908.

A NEW DIMENSION IN POLITICS

At first sight the Liberal Party leader, Sir Henry Campbell-Bannerman, seemed an unlikely revolutionary. Sixty-nine years old at the time of the 1906 election, he was a genial, avuncular figure, admired less as a parliamentary orator than as an efficient political operator who had held his party together in difficult times. Born Henry Campbell, the son of a successful Scottish merchant who rose to be Lord Provost of Glasgow, he had agreed to accept the second barrel to his name as a precondition of inheriting a rich uncle's legacy. He grew up within the Liberal fold, was an MP by the age of 32 and went on to serve as Gladstone's Chief Secretary for Ireland then subsequently as Secretary for War, before being chosen to head the party in 1899. A Europhile before the term was invented, he spent at least six weeks on the Continent each summer, regularly frequenting Edward VII's favourite spa, Marienbad. Otherwise he divided his time between London and Perthshire, where he had a small estate. There, he indulged a fondness for animals, keeping a long-lived African grey parrot and, in his later days, some 30 French bulldogs.

TAKING THE CASE TO THE PEOPLE
The Liberal landslide of January 1906 was something of a self-inflicted wound for the Conservatives, whose leader, Arthur Balfour, had chosen to step down from office in December 1905 with almost two years of his term still to run. Balfour gambled that the Liberals would be too busy arguing among themselves to form an interim government while an election was called, but far from splitting the opposition, the call to office drew the Liberal Party together. Would-be MPs, like the Liberal candidate campaigning below, took their message to the voters with enthusiasm and conviction. The Liberals won in a landslide, gaining a 241-seat majority over their chief rivals, the Conservative and Liberal Unionists, and a clear majority in the Commons overall. They viewed the result as a mandate for social change. As for Balfour, he lost his seat in Manchester East and had to wait for a safe Tory seat to come up in the City of London to be re-elected to Parliament.

CB, as he was known to his colleagues, has a claim to be Britain's first Prime Minister, as the term, used informally for many years, only received official recognition shortly after he took office. Although he was in charge for little more than two years, he proved a competent leader with an astute and generous political brain behind his 'hail-fellow-well-met' manner. Early in his stewardship, he signalled his mastery of the Commons with a devastating attack on his predecessor, Arthur Balfour, freshly re-seated after suffering defeat in Manchester in the main election. 'He comes back', CB told assembled MPs, 'with the same airy graces, the same subtle dialectics, the same light and frivolous way of dealing with great questions. He little knows the temper of the new House of Commons if he thinks these methods will prevail here … I say, enough of this foolery!'

The attack struck home because the mood of Parliament had indeed changed. Balfour himself admitted as much when he wrote to an acquaintance: 'What is going on here is a faint echo of the same movement which has produced massacres in St Petersburg, riots in Vienna and Socialist processions in Berlin.' No such revolutionary dramas accompanied the Liberal takeover, but there was a feeling that the old order was crumbling. As J B Priestley would one day put it, 'this 1906 election took politics into a new dimension'.

Progressive Liberalism

The novelty in the progressive Liberalism that now came to the fore lay chiefly in its willingness to look to the state to set social policy. The expanding appetite for bigger government drew on many sources. A growing awareness of the plight of the poor played a part, sparked by the writings of Charles Booth and Seebohm Rowntree, and by the sorry condition of many Boer War recruits. Equally important was the belief, shared by some members on the Conservative side of the House, that Britain was falling behind its foreign competitors – in particular Germany. There, the impeccably unradical Chancellor Otto von Bismarck had already introduced old-age pensions and health and accident insurance for workers, not so much out of compassion for their plight as from fear that they might otherwise turn to Socialism. Winston Churchill, re-elected to parliament in the 1906 election as a Liberal MP, had Bismarck's example very much in mind when he argued that 'the minister who applies to this country the successful experience of Germans in social organisation may or may not be supported at the polls, but he will at least have a memorial which time will not deface'.

The result was a growing conviction that the government would have to take a lead in protecting the weak and providing for those who could not look after themselves. Earlier administrations had been fearful of state intervention – even in times of emergency. When famine in India threatened millions with starvation in 1900, Balfour had turned down requests for additional aid on the grounds that it would encourage 'financial irregularity and extravagance … the most fruitful parent of social troubles'. The parliamentary class of 1906 were less concerned with balancing budgets than with the need to address fundamental flaws in the nation's social fabric. Reform was the order of the day.

LIBERAL LEADER
Described by an admirer as 'a gay old dog with a twinkle in his eye', the new Liberal Prime Minister Sir Henry Campbell-Bannerman was a committed reformer. His taste for the good life also enabled him to establish an easy rapport with Edward VII, helping to reconcile the King to the new government's radical programme. In the event CB's short premiership was dogged by ill health, which forced him to resign from office in April 1908. Too sick to move from No 10 Downing Street, he died there three weeks later, the only former prime minister to do so.

This new-found zeal for changing the status quo did not at first extend to Ireland. Remembering too well the divisions of Gladstone's day, Campbell-Bannerman's administration limited itself to continuing Balfour's work of mild reform, introducing measures to encourage the use of the Irish language, to establish an Irish national university, and to improve primary education and housing. Government motivation for more radical change would not reappear until 1910, when the Liberals, re-elected as a minority government, became dependent once more on the support of Irish MPs – and Home Rule became a pressing issue.

Children's Charter

In marked contrast, the reformers passionately embraced the cause of disadvantaged children across Britain, producing a body of legislation sometimes referred to collectively as the Children's Charter. In 1906 an act of parliament encouraged local authorities to provide free meals for needy pupils. The following year compulsory medical examinations were introduced in schools. Then, in 1908, came the Children Act, a wide-ranging piece of legislation designed to prevent the

PICKING UP BAD HABITS
A young girl shares a drink in a pub (left), while young strawberry-pickers puff away on cigarettes during a work break (above). Juvenile drinking and smoking were major causes of concern. The Band of Hope, a temperance movement, had some 2 million supporters by 1900; its campaigning helped to persuade the Conservative government to ban the sale of alcohol, unless in a sealed container, to children under 14. Smoking was considered a prime cause of 'physical deterioration', a leading social issue of the day, and groups like the Boys' Brigade and International Anti-Cigarette League had members sign pledges to refrain from the habit. The Liberal government took up the cause in the Children Act of 1908, which included measures banning young people from entering pubs or buying tobacco.

NANNY STATE

Nannies were a fixture in affluent families in the Edwardian years, taking on not just the physical, but also often the emotional demands of motherhood. Nannies were officially known as 'nurses' and their domain was the nursery, where they sometimes had a subordinate nurserymaid to help them. In the grander aristocratic houses, nannies often remained in attendance for decades on end, raising successive generations until they finally became a permanent – and often much-loved – part of the household. In such circumstances it was not uncommon for children to grow up feeling closer to their nanny, who looked after them, than to their actual mother or father, who might well be distant figures whom they saw only occasionally. Winston Churchill had such an upbringing. When, during a stay in the USA, he heard that his old nurse was dying, he returned immediately to England to see her. He wrote in his journal at the time, 'She was my favourite friend'.

'Edwardian nannies had no days off; they would not expect to go out and leave their charges to anyone else, except perhaps the nursery maid … and then only for a short while.'

Thea Thompson, *Edwardian Childhoods*

LEARNING A TRADE

A class of boys learn carpentry under the watchful eye of masters in a manual training centre. Vocational training was a much-neglected aspect of Britain's educational system. The old model of compulsory apprenticeships had fallen into disuse early in the previous century, and no comprehensive scheme for teaching young people the skills to earn a living had replaced it. For the most part youngsters either followed in their fathers' footsteps or else learned on the job in whatever trade they could find. The Education Act of 1902 placed the vocational element of schooling, like all others, under the control of local education authorities, and some took the opportunity to open facilities attached to primary schools where older pupils could learn useful, saleable job skills. Such centres were the exception rather than the rule, and most school leavers simply had to fend for themselves.

exploitation of the young on a variety of fronts. One section introduced the registration of foster parents, hoping thereby to discourage the long-established custom of baby-farming. Others prevented children from working in dangerous trades, from entering public houses and from purchasing cigarettes or fireworks.

The criminal justice system, which had previously drawn little distinction between adult and juvenile offenders, received a thorough makeover. To reduce the risk of the young being corrupted by their elders in crime, special courts were set up to handle juvenile cases. Those found guilty might be sent to reformatories, following a model already tested at a prison in Kent. Called Borstals, after the village where the prototype was situated, the new institutions were intended to emphasise education as much as punishment in a strictly regimented daily routine. One early inmate later recalled the regime with a grudging respect; there was plenty of outdoor exercise, he learned woodworking in the carpenter's shop, and was introduced to Dickens through a copy of *Oliver Twist* in the prison library.

The Children's Charter had lasting significance for the treatment of the young in Britain, but it formed only one part of the Liberal programme. The reformers also set their sights on improving the lot of working men and their families, particularly the old and the sick. The most insistent voices for change came from another political group that emerged greatly strengthened from the 1906 election – the Labour Representation Committee (LRC), soon to be renamed the Labour Party.

LABOUR ON THE RISE

For die-hard opponents of change, one of the most alarming aspects of the new intake of MPs was the return of 29 Labour members, a massive increase on the two MPs elected in the previous so-called Khaki Election of 1900. Traditionalists shook their heads in dismay. Lord Knollys, Edward VII's private secretary, privately noted that 'the old idea that the House of Commons was an assemblage of "gentlemen" has quite passed away'.

The Labour Representation Committee (LRC) had been born in February 1900 at a conference in London set up to provide a focus for the working-class vote that had emerged since the Reform Acts of 1867 and 1884. In the intervening years the trade unions had sponsored a number of MPs, mostly from mining constituencies, who cooperated with the radical wing of the Liberal Party and were sometimes referred to at the time as Lib-Labs. Another major current of support came from the ethical socialists whose chief mouthpiece was the Independent Labour Party (ILP), founded in 1893 by Keir Hardie and others. These idealists drew on the thoughts of John Ruskin, William Morris and similar reformers. The LRC drew less long-term support from the Marxist-oriented Social Democratic Foundation, which initially joined up to the cause but dropped out after a year. It also had limited influence from the Fabian Society, a left-wing intellectual powerhouse at the time under the influence of Sidney and Beatrice Webb and the

WORKING MAN'S VOTE

The Labour Party became a force in the Edwardian era thanks to its success in mobilising the working-class vote enfranchised by the electoral reform acts of 1867 and 1884. At first the Liberals were the main beneficiaries of these measures, but the conviction gradually spread that the interests of the working class would be best served by a political party of their own. One crucial factor was the Taff Vale decision, which in 1901 made trade unions legally liable for profits lost through strike action. Another was the economic insecurity that workers faced in the years before unemployment pay or sickness benefit became available. The Cornishmen seen below eating their lunch at the Dolcoath Mine outside Camborne in Cornwall would have been only too aware of potential threats to their future. The mine had been worked since the early 18th century, for copper at first and then primarily tin. But by Edwardian times there was growing competition from cheaper providers in other parts of the world. Tin prices would collapse after the First World War, leading to Dolcoath's closure in 1921.

THE VOICE OF LABOUR

Keir Hardie, seen here with beard and hat, campaigning for another Labour candidate in the 1906 election. Hardie was one of the founding fathers of the British Labour movement, first elected to Parliament in 1892 as the first, independent, socialist MP. He helped to found the Independent Labour Party, becoming its first leader, and played a crucial role in setting up the Labour Representation Committee – forerunner of the Labour Party – as an autonomous, working-class political body separate from the Liberals. In 1906 he was returned to Parliament as MP for Merthyr Tydfil. In his day Hardie took some controversial stances – he was an outspoken pacifist during the Boer War, and also supported women's suffrage – that made him something of a hate figure for his political opponents; it was said of him that 'no speaker had more meetings broken up'.

playwright George Bernard Shaw, which preferred to concentrate its efforts on influencing government policy outside Parliament. In any event, in the wake of their success in the 1906 election, the LRC members decided to change their name to the Labour Party.

The Taff Vale ruling

The biggest boost that the nascent parliamentary movement received came, ironically, from its enemies. In 1900 men working for the Taff Vale Railway Company in South Wales went on strike, unofficially at first but later, after the company hired blackleg replacements, with union backing. The management responded by bringing an action against the Amalgamated Society of Railway Servants for the losses incurred as a result of the action. The case went all the way to the Law Lords, who decided in 1901 in the company's favour, awarding damages of £23,000 and costs totalling a further £19,000 – a huge sum at the time, equivalent to some £3 million today.

The judgment had huge implications for the unions, which had previously considered themselves safe from law suits on the grounds that they were not incorporated in the manner of businesses. The Taff Vale precedent suggested that

continued on page 106

WORKSHOP OF THE WORLD

Despite fears about the growing competition from Germany and the USA, Edwardian Britain remained the workshop of the world; as late as 1914 the nation still had a 31 per cent share of international trade in manufactured goods, larger than that of any other country. In Lancashire and the West Riding of Yorkshire, around Birmingham and Glasgow and Tyneside, factory chimneys still dominated the urban skyline as they had done for half a century and more. For the most part industry was still in the hands of family firms, but the factories themselves had grown in size as steam replaced water as the principal power source. Life was hard for the workers within them, but it was still better than the prospect of joblessness outside.

The census of 1901 showed that a third of Britain's workers laboured in manufacturing. Between them, they produced almost three-quarters of the nation's total output.

MACHINE AGE
Manufacturing in Britain remained highly localised in Edwardian times. The Potteries region of Staffordshire was famous for ceramic production, while Sheffield specialised in metalwork, particularly cutlery. Lancashire was home to the textile industry, which extended across the county line into Yorkshire; one of the biggest mills was Crossley's in Halifax, employing more than 5,000 people. Hosiery was in the East Midlands, while London hosted a variety of manufactures including instrument-making and the burgeoning business of electrical engineering. Many industrial towns shared a profile of big industrial buildings, factory chimneys and cramped terraced housing, as displayed by this Lancashire mill town (left) – an urban landscape that would one day be immortalised by the painter L S Lowry. Inside the factories, conditions had improved since early Victorian days, but remained harsh. Workers in the cotton mills, like this young boy operating a giant spinning mule (right), put up with almost unbearable noise levels and often went barefoot because of the heat and slippery floors.

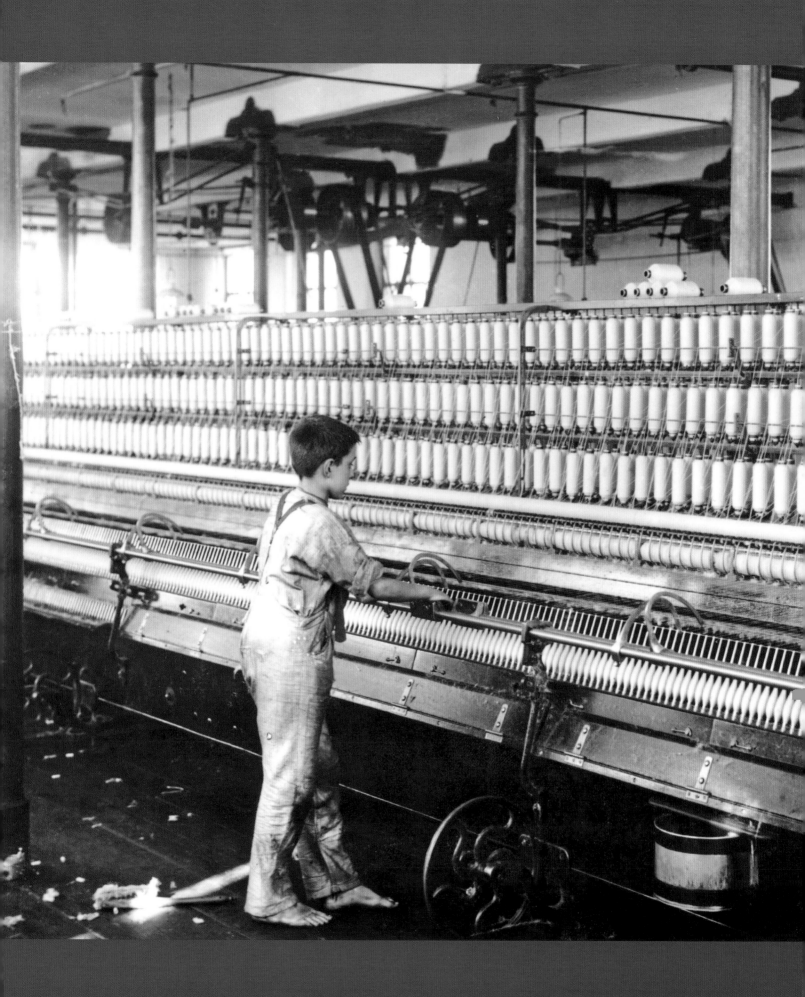

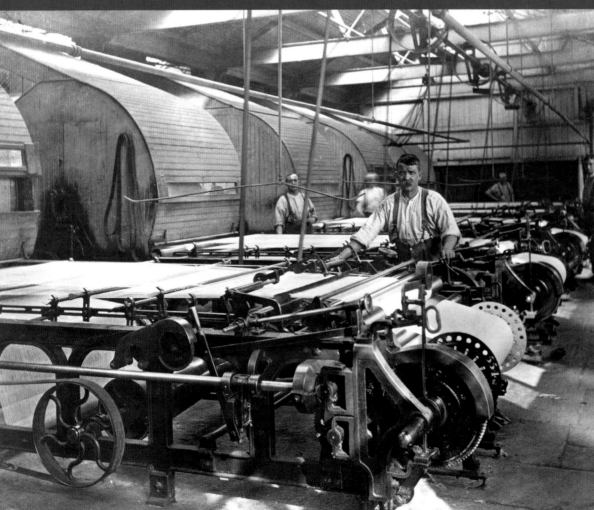

DOWN THE MILL

No branch of industry was more important to Britain than textiles, which accounted for almost half of all the nation's exports. It was also one of the biggest employers; the 1901 census revealed that more than 1.15 million people worked in the mills, more than half of them women. The most important part of the trade, making up over 50 per cent of total textile output, was the manufacture of cotton, which was largely concentrated in Lancashire. The mills here had been a driving force in the mechanisation and modernisation of industry. These women (top left) are operating looms in the winding room of one such mill, while the men below are preparing the warp on weaving looms at Horrock's, Crewdon & Co in Preston, an establishment that claimed to be 'the greatest cotton mills in the world'.

While cotton was the biggest, it was not the only important textile trade in Britain. The West Riding of Yorkshire was a centre for wool and worsted, while Belfast was famously a hub of linen production. These men (right) were photographed at work in a Belfast linen mill in about 1900, by which time the city was the linen capital of the world. Indeed, the the proliferation of linen mills was the driving force behind the growth of the city, which had outstripped Dublin in population by 1891.

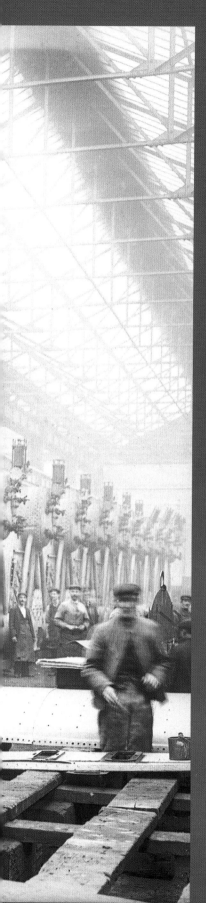

MEN'S WORK

In Edwardian days, as now, heavy industry was a male domain. Of almost 1 million people employed in the sector in 1901, just 54,000 were women. Many workers toiled in large plants, like these men in the boiler manufacturing area of the Yarrow shipyard at Poplar in London's East End (left). But there were also plenty of opportunities in smaller machine rooms, like this one (above) in a factory in Burnley. The aristocrats of the workforce were the skilled mechanics employed in workshop industries, and it was generally accepted that men were better at such work than women. This unashamedly sexist 1906 advert for Triumph boasts proudly of the fact that their bicycles were produced entirely by men, proclaiming Triumph to be 'the only Coventry cycle factory not employing female labour'.

Triumph CYCLES

MALE OR FEMALE LABOUR.

The male mechanic in the Workshop has proved himself infinitely superior to the female— he is capable of doing better, more exact, more reliable work.

Morally, mixed labour does not raise the standard of either worker, and considerably lowers the standard of the work produced.

TRIUMPH Cycles are made in a factory where no female labour whatever is employed. Female labour and best work do not go together therefore let your machine be a **TRIUMPH.** "The Best Bicycle British Workmanship can produce" and made by skilled male mechanics only.

The **TRIUMPH** is the only Coventry Cycle Factory not employing female labour.

£6 14s. 9d. to **£17 4s. 6d.**

Gradual payments from 10/8 Monthly.

Motors from £30.

Art Catalogues Post Free. Agents Everywhere.

Triumph Cycle Co. Ltd. (Dept. G 5), Coventry. Est. 1885.

London: 4-5 Holborn Viaduct, E.C. Leeds: 4, King Edward St. Manchester: 160, Deansgate.

FACTORY WORK FOR WOMEN

In 1901 nearly a third of British women had regular jobs, with the highest proportion of female employment being concentrated in the major textile centres. The only places to rival the mill towns in the numbers of women employed were Bournemouth and Bath, which both had an unusually high demand for maids and cooks. Across the nation as a whole, domestic service was still the most common source of work, accounting for over 40 per cent of all female employment; in comparison, 14 per cent worked in the textile industry and 8 per cent in other manufacturing.

Conditions and rewards were poor by modern standards; a 1906 Board of Trade survey found that women workers in industry earned on average less than 10 shillings (50p) for a 54-hour week. Even so, that was better than the 80-hour week worked by some shop assistants at the time, some of whom, as a condition of employment, had to live in dormitories above their work. The result was that there was rarely a shortage of applicants for factory jobs, no matter how boring the task. The women at top left are employed as button-cutters, while the tightly packed rows of women at bottom left are hand-rolling cigarettes in a Manchester factory. Many women were employed in some sort of garment manufacture: the women at centre left are making men's caps with the aid of sewing machines. The main picture (right) shows women at work hand-crafting hats at the Sutton & Torkington factory, also in Manchester. Almost without exception they are immaculately turned out for work, wearing clothes that they most likely sewed themselves at home.

in future any kind of industrial action might be ruinously expensive. Politically, the result was to drive much of the labour movement into the welcoming arms of the LRC, which made it a political priority to introduce legislation to reverse the judgment. In the two years that followed the Taff Vale ruling, union affiliation to the new body more than doubled, from 350,000 to 850,000.

`The first Lib-Lab pact
The next step in the Labour Party's rise came in 1903, when the LRC formed an electoral pact with the Liberals. Both parties agreed not to put up candidates against the other in constituencies where either one had a decisive advantage.

THE BACKBONE OF INDUSTRY
Smoke rises above the Wattstown Mine in the Rhondda Valley in 1905. Coal mining was a vital contributor to national prosperity, with output steadily rising to reach a peak of 290 million tons in 1913. All the traditional colliery areas were still producing, but growth was fastest in the more recently developed coalfields of Yorkshire, Wales and the East Midlands. There, as elsewhere, miners tended to live in tight-knit communities, with their own customs and a strong sense of local solidarity. The work was fairly well-paid by the standards of the day, yet few people outside the industry chose to go down the pits, put off by the prospect of labouring long hours deep underground in dirty, dark and dangerous conditions. An awareness of the arduous nature of the job contributed to the passing of the Mines (Eight Hours) Act in 1908, the first piece of legislation to limit working hours for adult men.

Never popular with activists, the move was nonetheless effective: in the 1906 election, out of 32 of the LRC's 50 nominations who stood unopposed by Liberals, 24 – more than two thirds – won their seats. This compared with less than a third – five successful candidates from 18 – among those who faced Liberal opponents, sometimes in the form of unofficial independents.

As Lord Knollys duly noted, the new crop of Labour MPs did not fit existing preconceptions of the nation's elected representatives. All were from working-class backgrounds and most had trade union affiliations. There was also a strong Non-conformist presence. Between them, they brought to the House a first-hand knowledge of conditions in the poorer parts of Britain, giving added immediacy to the drive for reform. It was a Labour member, for instance, who introduced the free school meals measure as a private member's bill that subsequently gained government backing.

The Labour MPs also repaid their debt to their backers by pushing through the Trade Disputes Act. This reversed the Taff Vale judgment and gave the unions an extraordinary degree of immunity from prosecution for any form of peaceful picketing. At first the Liberal Cabinet preferred a less radical measure, but when Campbell-Bannerman himself spoke up for a stronger bill put forward by one of

continued on page 111

DEATH IN THE MINES – WAITING FOR NEWS

Work in the pits was unhealthy at the best of times, but all too often it could be lethal. Mining disasters were a regular occurrence in the Edwardian years, and they took a heavy toll. In 1901 a gas explosion at the East Side Pit in Senghenydd, north of Cardiff, claimed 83 lives. Four years later 119 were killed at the Wattstown Mine in the Rhondda Valley (see photograph, page 107), in the worst mining disaster in Wales for more than a decade. In March 1908 a fire broke out at the Hamstead Colliery near Birmingham (right), killing 25 of the 31 miners underground at the time; the photograph shows the pithead vigil of families waiting for news of husbands, sons, fathers and brothers. There were similar scenes five months later when word spread around the village of Abram, outside Wigan, of an underground explosion at the local Maypole Colliery. Again, there was little cheer for waiting relatives (below); 75 men died in the explosion and ensuing fire, while only three were rescued. Worse was to come before the decade was out. In 1909, at the Burns Pit in West Stanley, Durham, explosions and fire killed 168 miners; the only relief for the rescuers was being able to bring out several pit ponies alive. And just before Christmas 1910, the Pretoria Pit near Westhoughton and Atherton became the scene of the worst-ever mining disaster in Lancashire, when 344 were killed. Such disasters occurred despite the best efforts of mine managers, inspectors and union representatives. Their effects were devastating on the close-knit communities involved. Often several members of a family were killed in a disaster, and often, too, boys as young as 13 died.

RESCUE GEAR

Mining disasters brought out a deep sense of solidarity in the communities they affected, and there was never any shortage of volunteers to undertake the dangerous job of trying to rescue survivors. Rescue teams first had to overcome the problem of access, as the pit cages were often put out of action by the explosions. Below ground the teams faced the threat of roof falls, as well as inhaling smoke and dust. Afterdamp – a poisonous gas consisting mostly of carbon monoxide that formed in the wake of explosions – posed a particular danger. To combat the threat, some rescuers donned Draegar smoke helmets (below) reminiscent of the gear used by deep-sea divers; invented in Germany in 1903, the helmets were available at the time of the 1908 Hamstead Colliery fire. Another difficulty lay in removing the injured and the dead; this stretcher on wheels (right), on display at a mining rescue school, was designed to help.

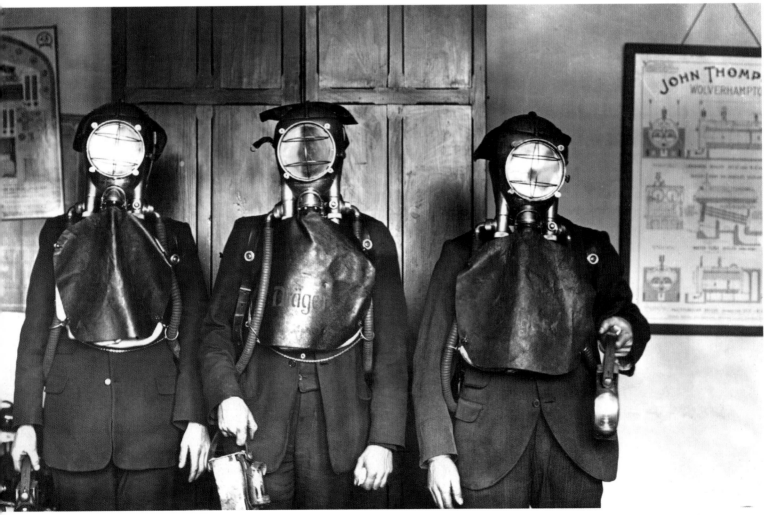

the trade-union sponsored MPs, the House swung behind it and it was voted into law against the advice of the government's own Attorney General. Other welfare measures that the new parliamentary Labour group helped to pass into law included the Workmen's Compensation Act, which improved the benefits payable to people injured at work and provided relief in cases of industrial disease, and the Mines Act, which introduced an eight-hour working day for miners down the pits.

Challenges from left and right

Despite these successes, the Labour movement encountered many obstacles on its path to parliamentary power. Left-wing socialists objected to the compromises involved in working alongside the Liberals. They found a spokesman in Victor Grayson, a fiery orator from Liverpool. Nominated by the Independent Labour Party as its candidate for a by-election in Colne Valley, the 26-year-old was asked to stand down by the Labour executive under the terms of the Lib-Lab pact. He refused and put himself forward instead as an Independent Socialist. To the astonishment of the party leadership, he pipped the Liberal candidate at the post, winning by 153 votes on an 88 per cent turnout. But thereafter Grayson spent little time in the House of Commons, preferring to spread the socialist message at public meetings. On one occasion when he did attend a parliamentary debate, he intervened to accuse the House of ignoring the plight of the unemployed and was removed by the Serjeant-at-Arms – but not before rounding on the other Labour members, accusing them of being traitors to their class.

Sharing power with the Liberals also cost Labour support when the economy, which had been doing well, entered a downturn. By 1908 unemployment was a growing concern, having risen to 7.8 per cent from the average of 5 per cent that it had been for most of the decade. The slowdown was already hurting the party when, in 1909, another hostile judgment was meted out by the Law Lords. The secretary of the Walthamstow branch of the Amalgamated Society of Railway Servants, one W V Osborne, was a Liberal voter who had taken exception to the fact that the union was using his dues, along with those of all its other members, to subsidise the Labour Party. He took his case to court and eventually it reached the House of Lords, where it was decided that the unions' political levy was indeed illegal. The ruling hit the Labour MPs hard – they depended on the trade union contributions to pay their salaries. The judgment was overturned by fresh legislation in 1913, but in the intervening period the party's finances nose-dived.

Yet for all its difficulties, Labour went on to increase its share of the vote from 4.8 to over 7 per cent in the January 1910 election. It also gained more seats, raising its presence in the Commons to 40 MPs, although most of the new intake could be put down to the decision of the Miners' Federation to affiliate with the party, bringing the sponsored MPs who had previously stood as Lib-Labs under the Labour umbrella. A further election in December 1910 actually saw the Labour share of the national vote drop to 6.3 per cent, but concentrated local support for the party in industrial areas saw its number of MPs go up again, this time to 42 seats. Overall it was an impressive showing for the young party; over the course of the decade it had seen its direct membership increase by more than half to 35,000 while the number of workers in affiliated trade unions reached 1.4 million. By 1910 Labour had established itself as a prominent feature of Britain's parliamentary democracy, even if few people could have guessed at the time that it would eclipse its Liberal partners in little more than a decade.

MOTOR CARS AND FLYING MACHINES

For all the changes the Liberal victory set in motion, the most profound transformation at work in the first decade of the 20th century was, as H G Wells had foreseen, the transport revolution. Between 1900 and 1910 the nation entered the motor age. Automobiles were not new. The days when road locomotives had by law to be preceded by a man waving a red flag were already long gone. By 1901 there were an estimated 10,000 motor vehicles in the country, and they were allowed to power along the nation's highways at a dizzying 14mph. The new form of locomotion acquired an important ally when Edward VII came to the throne, for the King was himself a keen motorist.

To celebrate motoring's growing reliability, in April 1900 the Automobile Club of Great Britain organised the One Thousand Mile Trial, a test of stamina that saw 65 vehicles leave Hyde Park Corner in London on a tour that took in every major city in England and Scotland. All 65 managed to complete the course, although there were many tribulations on the way. One competitor negotiated the

CARS COME OF AGE
Scheduled over three weeks in April and May 1900, the Thousand Mile Trial was a great success. Crowds turned out in all the major cities of England and Scotland to cheer on the entrants, like the cars below photographed just outside St Albans on the return leg. The front Panhard is driven by Frank Hedges Butler, a balloonist and pioneer aviator, as well as early motorist. The aim of the event was to familiarise the public with cars and to trumpet the start of the motor age, and to judge from results it was hugely successful. By the decade's end the number of vehicles on the roads had rocketed from around 10,000 to over 80,000, and a market had grown up for motoring clothes and paraphernalia, such as the motor bonnet for ladies advertised in 1905 (below right). Although driving was still a hobby for the wealthy, like the actress Isabel Jay seen at the wheel of a Dutch-made Spyker in 1907 (right), the first mass-produced Fords would soon arrive from the USA and by the end of the decade the age of mass motoring was on the way.

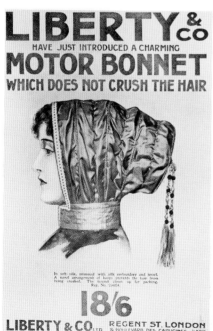

LIBERTY & CO
HAVE JUST INTRODUCED A CHARMING
MOTOR BONNET
WHICH DOES NOT CRUSH THE HAIR

In soft silk, trimmed with silk embroidery and tassel. A novel arrangement of hoops prevents the hair from being crushed. The bonnet shown up for packing. Reg. No. 554654.

18/6

LIBERTY & CO. LTD **REGENT ST. LONDON** & BOULEVARD DES CAPUCINES PARIS

last 52 miles without any steering – his passenger had to stand on the running board and kick the front wheels when the vehicle needed to change direction.

The increasing number of automobiles on the roads convinced Balfour's government of a need for fresh legislation. The Motor Car Act of 1903 made dangerous driving an offence and introduced vehicle registration, organised at the time through county councils, making it illegal for anyone but the King to drive a car without a licence plate. Drivers, too, had in future to obtain licences, although by the simple expedient of paying the council five shillings (25p).

In the years that followed the popularity of motoring continued to grow, for the most part as a recreation for the rich. The process of democratisation, opening up the roads to the middle classes, only really got under way after 1908, when the first cheap Fords were imported from the USA. In the meantime, dozens of motoring enthusiasts had set up small manufacturing plants in provincial factories and backstreet workshops, all hoping to establish a toehold in the new market. In total, 198 different makes of automobile would be offered for sale in Britain between 1900 and 1913. Most quickly failed.

Enter Rolls-Royce

One glorious exception was the Rolls-Royce company, which built its reputation on the engineering skills of Henry Royce. The son of a failed miller who had died in Henry's childhood, Royce supplemented his family's income first by selling newspapers and delivering telegrams and then by taking up an apprenticeship with

TESTING THEIR METTLE
As cars became more reliable and mechanically more sophisticated, their makers and owners sought ways of testing their capabilities to the limits, and so motor sports were born. The first Tourist Trophy (TT) races were held on the Isle of Man in 1905, the location chosen to escape the speed limits that applied on the mainland. The fourth meeting of the series, staged in 1908, has gone down in motoring history as the 'Four-Inch Race', because regulations aimed at attracting cars of Grand Prix calibre stipulated that all competing vehicles must have a four-cylinder engine with a maximum bore size of 4in. Kenelm Lee Guinness (left) failed to finish in his Hillman-Coatalen, although his brother Algernon came second; the winning Napier-Hutton averaged more than 50mph during the race. Motor trials were also popular, serving as long-distance endurance tests (right). The photograph shows a competitor in the 1906 Scottish trials negotiating the notorious Devil's Elbow, a hairpin bend on the Cairnwell Pass between Glenshee and Braemar.

the Great Northern Railway, paid for by a kindly aunt. He came to cars by way of electrical engineering, producing his first prototypes in 1904. One came to the attention of the Honourable Charles Rolls, an aristocratic automobile salesman with premises in London's West End who was looking for a new model to supplement the imported French Panhards he sold. The two men met in the Midland Hotel, Manchester, and agreed to form a partnership.

The rest of the story is automotive history. The first Rolls-Royce car made its debut at the Paris Motor Show in December 1904. Two years later the firm of Rolls-Royce Ltd was officially incorporated, and by the following year was winning prizes for reliability. In 1908 the firm moved to a larger factory in Derby, and a legendary British marque was up and running.

Motor racing and other developments

By that time motor transport was moving into a new era of sophistication and speed. The Royal Automobile Club, graced by Edward VII's patronage, began organising the Tourist Trophy (TT) road races on the Isle of Man in 1905. The first event was won by John S Napier at an average speed of almost 34mph; a year later the victor was Charles Rolls, always a keen tester of his firm's products. In 1907 the banked Brooklands motor-racing circuit was opened in Surrey, and by the following year cars were lapping at over 100mph, although five more years would pass before a vehicle could sustain that pace for a full 60 minutes.

By 1910 the number of cars on Britain's roads had soared to over 83,000 and, just as significantly, the petrol engine had been adapted to many other uses.

continued on page 118

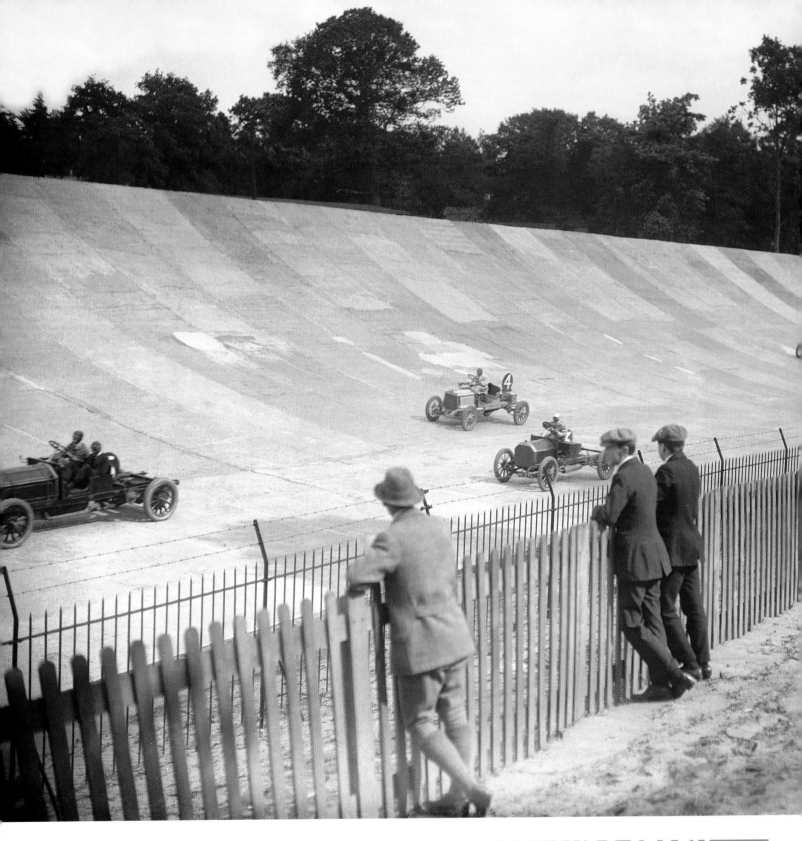

A DAY AT THE RACES – THE BROOKLANDS STORY

When the Brooklands circuit opened near Weybridge in Surrey in 1907, it was the world's first purpose-built motor racetrack, beating the Indianapolis Speedway in the USA by over a year. Its most distinctive feature was the banking, in places almost 30ft (9m) in height, which allowed drivers to reach otherwise unattainable speeds when cornering. For reasons of economy, the track was made of concrete rather than asphalt, making for a bumpy ride in later years. Eleven days after the circuit opened, Selwyn Edge (bottom right) – an Australian entrepreneur who had won the Automobile Club's Thousand Mile Trial in 1900 – staged a celebrated 24-hour event, leading three Napier cars in a round-the-clock endurance trial. Taking no breaks, Edge covered more than 1580 miles at an average speed of over 65mph. Thereafter the Brooklands track became a venue for

more conventional motor races like the 1908 contest seen above, as well as motorcycle trials. One unusual feature by present-day standards was the presence of elegantly dressed bookies (top right) offering competitive odds. In the Second World War Brooklands served as an airfield, and no further racing took place thereafter. Today a motor-racing and aviation museum occupies part of the site.

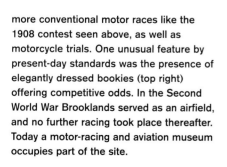

The first British motorcycles had appeared at the start of the decade. In 1902 a manufacturer in Biggleswade produced the earliest commercially successful tractor, a three-wheeled model that was at first shunned by traditionalist farmers for its inability to produce manure. Motor taxis arrived in 1903 and by 1910 they were a common sight in cities, as were motor buses, supplementing the electric trams that had been part of the urban scene for a decade.

The electrification of the London Underground, begun in the 1890s, was well under way, replacing the old steam-driven locomotives and powering the new, deeper lines that were coming into use to meet the needs of the capital's growing army of commuters. The Central Line opened between Bank and Shepherd's Bush stations in 1900, and the Northern Line extension up to Hampstead opened in 1907. A comparison of journey times that year found the trip from Piccadilly Circus to Baker Street on the newly opened Bakerloo Line took 7 minutes at a cost of twopence (less than 1p); the omnibus cost the same but took 20 minutes; and a horse-drawn cab arrived in 15 minutes, but set the passenger back 1s 6d (7.5p).

By no means everyone welcomed the noise and smells of the new motor age. The novelist E M Forster thought cars 'pestilential' and complained that, rather than liberating people, science had enslaved them to machines. The Marquis of Queensberry, famous for his eccentricities, stated on an application for a firearms licence that he needed a shotgun to shoot motorists using the roads on his estate.

MOTOR TAXI RANK
Taxis line up at a cab rank alongside London's Hyde Park in 1907. Electrically-powered vehicles, nicknamed 'Hummingbirds' for the noise they made, had been introduced experimentally in 1897, but they proved unreliable and were withdrawn three years later. The first petrol-powered cabs appeared on the capital's streets in 1903. At first they struggled to compete with the familiar horse-drawn hansoms, but that situation changed dramatically in late 1906 when the General Cab Company put 500 vehicles, made in France by Renault, into commission. The public quickly got the habit of using the new-fangled conveyances, and by 1910 motor cabs outnumbered their horse-drawn rivals by 6,300 to 5,000.

SPEED ON TWO WHEELS
Motorised bicycles powered by petrol engines first began to appear as early as the mid-1880s. By 1902 the Triumph Company was producing machines in Britain fitted with Belgian-made engines. By 1907 motorcycle racing had become an established sport, and in that year the first TT race for bikes was held on a 15-mile road course in the Isle of Man. The winning machine was a Matchless, similar to the one shown below lining up the following year at an Essex Motor Club meeting; the TT winner completed the 10-lap, 150-mile race in a little over 4 hours at an average speed of 38.21mph. Accidents were common and injuries to riders were exacerbated by the complete lack of safety gear; as the photograph shows, racers did not even wear helmets or gloves.

Opponents of combustion engines sometimes took refuge in cycling, a passion of the old century that continued in the new. H G Wells, whose novel *The Wheels of Chance* was subtitled 'A Bicycling Idyll', was particularly eloquent in singing the praises of the new, low-slung safety bikes, as they opened the gates of the countryside for urban clerks and workers who might otherwise have never had a chance to know it. For long journeys the railways reigned supreme, and the number of passengers grew throughout the Edwardian era. Services were reliable and fast, with the 50-mile journey from London Victoria to Brighton, for example, taking just 53 minutes and comparing favourable with the journey time today.

Up, up and away
The great breakthrough of the decade was the advent of powered flight. The earliest pioneering ventures took place outside Britain, notably in the USA where the Wright brothers first achieved lift-off in December 1903. Their exploit aroused little interest locally at the time, with the *Daily Mail* merely noting on an inside page the trial of what it called a 'balloonless airship'. The first flight in the UK was not made until 1908, and then by an American, Samuel Franklin Cody, in a

continued on page 128

THE BIRTH OF FLIGHT

The concept of human flight was not new in 1900 – it had fascinated people since ancient times, and hot-air ballooning had been a vogue in France since before the French Revolution. Sir George Cayley and the German Otto Lilienthal had both had success experimenting with gliders in the 19th century. What still remained to be conquered as the 20th century dawned was powered directional flight, and the invention of the internal combustion engine in the 1880s provided the means. In 1903 Wilbur and Orville Wright achieved lift-off in a heavier-than-air machine, and the age of aviation was born. Few of the breakthrough developments took place in Britain, but even so it was not long before the nation was producing more than its share of talented and inventive aviators.

POWERED AIRSHIP
Aeroplanes were not the only focus of attention in the early years of flight. Inventors also sought ways of adapting hot-air balloons so they were not solely dependent on the wind for propulsion. The first airship designs were drawn up in the 18th century, and in 1852 a steam-powered model flew for 17 miles (27km). By the turn of the 20th century engineers were scrambling to come up with new designs. The model shown here (left) was the work of Britain's Stanley Spencer; 75ft (23m) long, it was powered by a petrol motor driving a front-mounted propeller.

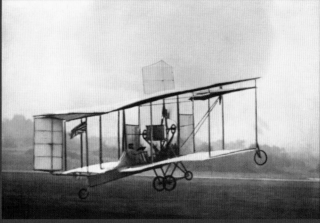

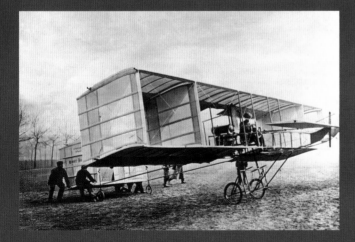

FIRST FLIGHTS

The Wright brothers' pioneering flight in 1903 set off a round of aviation records. The honour of making the first flight in Britain is usually given to the American Samuel Cody, a former Wild West Show showman who flew his Cody Aeroplane No.1 (top right) for 1500ft (450m) at Farnborough on 16 October, 1908. However, a claim of first flight in Britain is sometimes made for the truly bizarre 'Venetian Blind' Multiplane (top left) built by Horatio Phillips; it briefly achieved lift-off in 1907, but the plane lacked a steering mechanism. The first British aviator to fly a steerable machine is usually credited as John Moore-Brabazon, later Lord Brabazon of Tara, who flew 450ft (140m) in a French-made Farman–Voisin box-kite biplane (bottom left) on the Isle of Sheppey in April 1909. Another contender for both firsts was Alliott Verdon Roe, who flew a short, unofficial hop in his Roe 1 biplane (centre) at Brooklands in 1907. Roe can certainly claim the first flight in an all-British-made machine – his Avro Triplane (bottom right) in July 1909.

CROSSING THE CHANNEL

The first flight across the English Channel in a heavier-than-air machine was made on Sunday 25 July, 1909, by Frenchman Louis Blériot, flying a Blériot XI of his own design (left). Trained as an engineer, the 37-year-old had already amassed a small fortune inventing and manufacturing automobile headlamps before turning his attention to flying machines. His particular interest was in monoplanes – machines with a single set of wings, rather than the twin arrangement of biplanes – and he was credited with making the fist successful monoplane flight, in the Blériot V, in 1905. For his Channel hop, he took advantage of a pocket of clear weather and took off at dawn. Outstripping the French naval destroyer assigned to accompany him, he crash landed in wind and rain outside Dover at 05.20am, having flown 23.5 miles in 36.5 minutes. The solitary witness of the historic landing was a police constable, although onlookers gathered later to view the aviator and his plane (below).

SPECTATOR SPORT

The year 1909 was something of a breakthrough year in the history of aviation. Blériot's flight received widespread publicity, following on, as it did, from a celebrated series of demonstrations by the Wright brothers in the USA and Europe. The Wrights attracted worldwide attention, which only increased when Orville crashed from a height of 100ft (30m) in September 1908, injuring himself and killing his passenger. The new interest fuelled demand for public displays. In August 1909 an international aviation meeting at Reims in France hosted 38 different machines, while in England that October Blackpool hosted a Flying Week, the first officially recognised such meeting in Britain. The picture below shows the French aviator Henri Rougier demonstrating his skills in a biplane.

FAILED ATTEMPT
Blériot was not the only person
to respond to the challenge set
by the *Daily Mail*, which offered
a prize of £1,000 for the first
aviator to cross the Channel.
Six days before Blériot made
his historic flight another
Frenchman, Hubert Latham,
made the attempt in the
Antoinette IV monoplane shown
here. The craft suffered engine
failure halfway across and had
to put down in the water,
thereby making the first
recorded touchdown at sea.
Undeterred, Latham tried again
two days after Blériot, but had
to abandon the attempt when
his engine cut out once more.

'… as we tore along at
an increasing pace …
I expected to be jerked
and jolted. But the
motion was wonderfully
smooth – smoother yet –
and then, suddenly, there
had come into it a new,
indescribable quality – a
lift – a lightness – a life!'

Gertrude Bacon, pioneer aviator, describing lift-off in 1909,
in a flight piloted by French airman Roger Sommer

A POPULAR PASTIME – HOT-AIR BALLOONS

Even though the aviation community's attention was by now focused on powered craft, hot-air ballooning remained a popular pastime, attracting enthusiasts to events like this balloon race meeting at Hurlingham Park in London. The interest in balloons was not just recreational; aware of the value of aerial observation posts, the Royal Engineers maintained a balloon factory first at Aldershot and then at Farnborough, where a military airship was built in 1907. For most enthusiasts, though, the appeal of ballooning was entirely peaceful. One family who were particularly associated with the activity were the Spencers of London, one of whom designed the airship shown on page 120. The firm of C G Spencer & Sons made balloons for a variety of purposes, from advertising and aerial photography to public displays at fetes featuring parachute jumps and offering paid ascents.

machine he had designed for the British army. John Moore-Brabazon was the first Englishman to fly in English skies, achieving the feat in May 1909. Later that year he took a piglet up in his biplane to show that pigs could indeed fly.

By that time the *Daily Mail*'s owner, Lord Northcliffe, was an enthusiastic proponent of aviation. He announced two cash prizes: one of £1,000 for the first flight across the English Channel, the other of £10,000 for the first London-to-Manchester air journey. As it happened, both were won by Frenchmen. Louis Blériot successfully made the Channel hop in July 1909, completing the 23-mile trajectory in 37 minutes. The larger sum, not won until April 1910, went to Louis Paulhan after an epic contest with a British rival, Claude Grahame-White, both of them in planes built by Henri Farman. Following his victory Paulhan was feted at a victory dinner at London's Savoy Hotel, where the guests included H G Wells and Hiram Maxim, inventor of the eponymous machine-gun.

Just three months after Paulhan's success, the continuing dangers of early flight were graphically illustrated when Charles Rolls, by now a keen flyer, was killed crash-landing his biplane at an air display in Bournemouth. His death provided a grim epitaph for British aviation's rocky beginnings.

PIONEERS OF AVIATION
Dressed in a flat cap and breeches, the French aviator Henri Farman stands between two early British enthusiasts, the Roe brothers – Alliott Verdon on the left and Humphrey to the right. Farman was born in Paris of British parents, his father being a newspaper correspondent, and he became a racing cyclist and motor-racing driver before taking up aviation in 1907. Soon, he was modifying plane design to improve flight control, enabling him to fly the first circuits of 1km then 2km, followed by the first cross-country flight in Europe, from Chalons-sur-Marne to Rheims. Farman would become hugely influential in the development of the aviation industry, both in France and internationally. Alliott Roe was cast in the same mould. He and his brother would found the Avro aircraft company and build biplanes in the First World War.

THE ARTS – REFLECTING SOCIETY

After the 'Art for Art's Sake' aestheticism of the 1890s, writers and painters in the 1900s showed a new zest for the real world. Realism was in fact the order of the day, whether in the novels of Galsworthy, Wells and Arnold Bennett, the paintings of Walter Sickert, or the theatre of Harley Granville-Barker and George Bernard Shaw. All shared an interest in the texture of everyday life and a concern for the current, flawed condition of society.

Many of the writers and artists of the time were politically engaged, usually toward the left end of the spectrum (Rudyard Kipling being a notable exception). Some, like Shaw and, for a time, H G Wells, were deeply involved with the Fabian Society and its dream of building a socialist Britain. Others, like Galsworthy and Bennett, expressed support for Liberal social reform. Generally there was a feeling that the world could be changed – indeed, was crying out for transformation. Inequality and injustice would be uprooted and society shaped anew.

In keeping with the national mood, poetry went through something of a hiatus, with relatively little important new work appearing in the Edwardian years. In contrast, this was a great age for the novel. Henry James and Joseph Conrad were both producing important work to set beside that of the young social realists, who were setting the tone of the time. A defining characteristic of the younger generation was an emphasis on the workaday commercial and industrial middle classes – on store owners, shop assistants and clerks, like Wells's Kipps and Mr Polly, or the protagonists of Bennett's 'Five Towns' novels. Another was the assault on Victorian hypocrisy and evasion that informed Galsworthy's *Forsyte Saga*.

E M Forster, who produced all his major works except *A Passage to India* between 1905 and 1910, made snobbery and arrogance a central theme of his writing. The victims could be foreigners, as in *Where Angels Fear to Tread*, or the self-educated as in *A Room with a View*, or the struggling bank clerk Leonard Bast in *Howard's End*. In each case they fall foul of English social exclusiveness – only the young hero of *A Room with a View* has the energy, idealism and persistence to escape its meshes and win the girl he loves in face of her family's disapproval.

Against such closed horizons the novelists unfurled their human sympathies, producing vast panoramas of family life played out over a backdrop of passing decades. The masterpiece of the age was Arnold Bennett's *The Old Wives' Tale*, first published in 1908. It follows the lives of two sisters born in the Potteries from the cradle to the grave, spanning 70 years and arguably giving a more complete picture of the effects of the passage of time than any other British novel.

> 'Everybody got down off their stilts. Henceforward, nobody drank absinthe with their coffee. Nobody went mad. Nobody committed suicide. And nobody joined the Catholic Church.'
>
> W B Yeats, poet

A GOLDEN AGE FOR THE NOVEL

The novel was a forum for debate in Edwardian times, used by writers to assess and criticise the state of the nation. Two of the most successful authors of the day were John Galsworthy (top right) and Arnold Bennett (bottom right), who grounded their books in close observation of the workings of society. In his Forsyte novels, Galsworthy put the upper middle classes under the microscope, while Bennett's best work was rooted in the pottery towns of Staffordshire where he spent his childhood. E M Forster (top centre) shared their concern with relations between the classes, summing up his humanitarian belief in the need for communication in the simple phrase 'Only connect ...'. G K Chesterton (bottom centre) was quite as concerned with the state of the nation as any of the others, but approached the question from his own individualistic Christian viewpoint. A flamboyant and physically imposing figure – 6ft 4in (1.93m) tall and weighing over 20 stone (130kg) – he poured his immense energy into journalism, poems and short stories as well as novels, of which the best-known was the idiosyncratic *The Man who was Thursday*.

Neither Joseph Conrad (top left) nor Henry James (bottom left) were British-born, but they came to be regarded among the greatest exponents of the English novel. Conrad grew up in Poland and earned a living at sea before becoming a British citizen in 1886. His first novels appeared at the end of the 19th century; the Edwardian years would see some of his best work, including *Lord Jim*, *Nostromo* and *The Secret Agent*. American-born James had settled in London in 1876 and was already 57 when the decade began. In 1898 he moved to Rye on the south coast, where he bought the famous Lamb House, and continued to cement his literary reputation with new works, notably *The Wings of the Dove* (1902) and *The Ambassadors* (1903).

SOCIAL VISIONARY

George Bernard Shaw (right) was born in Dublin in 1856 and so was already 43 years old at the turn of the century. He came into his prime as a dramatist in the Edwardian years. Ten of his plays were staged at the Royal Court Theatre between 1904 and 1907, the first of which, *John Bull's Other Island*, made Edward VII laugh so hard he broke his chair. In 1906 Shaw and his wife moved to the house that would become known as Shaw's Corner in Ayot St Lawrence, Hertfordshire, where he lived for the rest of his life. He was a prolific writer, with more than 50 plays to his credit, and he is the only person to have won both a Nobel prize for literature and an Oscar. He was awarded – and reluctantly accepted – the Nobel prize in 1925; the Oscar came later, for the screenplay of *Pygmalion*.

Much of the Anglo-Irish playwright's boundless energy was spent on the social causes he espoused throughout his long life. He was an early member of the Fabian Society, dedicated to the cause of democratic socialism, and he wrote and edited many of the pamphlets published in its name. Shaw vigorously supported working-class representation in politics and attended the inaugural conference of the Independent Labour Party, a precursor of the Labour Party, helping Kier Hardie to write the party's programme. He campaigned vociferously for a variety of causes, ranging from equal rights for women to vegetarianism and a phonetic alphabet for the English language.

Dramatic developments

Similar social concerns were making themselves felt on stage, albeit for a minority audience. Then, as now, the great mass of theatre-goers viewed it as an excuse for a good night out, to be enjoyed after an early dinner or perhaps before a late supper à deux. The evening's entertainment might be a drawing-room comedy involving the complications of upper-class life, or perhaps one of the spectacular productions for which London's Drury Lane Theatre was especially famed – one play boasted not just a racetrack scene featuring six jockeys on mechanical horses, but also an on-stage train crash; another climaxed in an earthquake with houses collapsing and people (actually trained acrobats) leaping from windows. To see such extravaganzas fashionable London audiences paid as much as half a guinea (52.5p) for a seat in the stalls – roughly half a docker's weekly wage.

Such theatrical fare left the intelligentsia cold, and over the course of the decade they sought theatres prepared to stage more thought-provoking productions. One such place was London's Royal Court Theatre, where from 1904 to 1907 Harley Granville-Barker put on a ground-breaking series of plays, including no fewer than 10 works by George Bernard Shaw, the most influential playwright of the age.

HOME ENTERTAINMENT
A family gathers round a piano for a sing-song, enjoying one of the home pleasures that have largely disappeared in recent times. In the days before television and computer games, people were dependent on their own resources for much of their entertainment. In particular, at a time when the only available recorded music emerged scratchily from wax cylinders, most music-making was live. Besides domestic singalongs, music-lovers could hear brass bands in city parks during the summer months, and many people also enjoyed the social recreation of singing in choirs; even medium-sized towns hosted annual performances of Handel's 'Messiah' and other oratorios. Subscription concerts were another feature of the musical scene around the country; music-lovers would pay to attend a programme of concerts, rather in the manner of season-ticket holders at present-day sporting events.

Granville-Barker wrote plays of his own that touched on the same theme of corruption beneath the façade of respectability that attracted the novelists of the day. It was the banning of his play *Waste* – the plot shockingly involved a politician's adulterous affair and a botched abortion – that helped to inspire one of the great intellectual causes of the day. Dozens of influential writers, from Shaw and James Barrie to Henry James and Thomas Hardy, lent their support to the call to do away with the right of the Lord Chamberlain's office to censor plays. In response, Henry Campbell-Bannerman's Cabinet set up a parliamentary committee to consider the matter, but despite hearing the evidence of many leading writers and thinkers in favour of change, the committee eventually came down for the status quo. It would be 1968 before theatrical censorship was abolished.

Prodigious musical talents

Highbrow audiences seeking less politically challenging stimulation could always head for the concert halls. In the days before effective gramophones, let alone hi-fi, CDs or MP3 players, music remained a live art, and the classical genre was experiencing an explosion of talent. The Edwardian years saw some of Britain's best-loved composers either in their prime or exhibiting extraordinary early promise. Ralph Vaughan Williams composed his first major successes in the decade – 1910 saw acclaimed première performances of his 'Sea Symphony' and 'Fantasia on a Theme by Tallis'. Cheltenham-born Gustav Holst had yet to write 'The Planets', but he was producing compositions set to Sanskrit texts, reflecting an interest in Eastern mysticism, while earning a living as musical director of St Paul's Girl School and London's Morley College. Frederick Delius was based in France by this time, but was still producing works deeply influenced by English themes, such as 'In a Summer Garden' and 'Brigg Fair'. Folk collectors like Cecil Sharp and the Australian-born Percy Grainger were busy combing the countryside in search of the traditional songs that provided inspiration for such works.

The presiding genius of the Edwardian musical world was undoubtedly Sir Edward Elgar, whose compositions still, for many people, provide the mental soundtrack for the era. The decade began with his 'Cockaigne Overture', subtitled 'In London Town', but his most potent contribution of the time were the 'Pomp and Circumstance' marches, the first of which contained the setting for 'Land of Hope and Glory'. The march itself was an instant success: Henry Wood, who conducted the first London performance, recalled: 'The people simply rose and yelled. I had to play it again, with the same result. In fact they refused to allow me to get on with the programme.' According to Elgar, it was Edward VII who subsequently suggested that the tune be used as a setting for A C Benson's 'Coronation Ode', of which 'Land of Hope and Glory' was a part. Ironically, the composer would later claim never to have liked the words that he made into such an enduring part of the nation's heritage.

New realism in painting

In his appearance and habits, Elgar was very much an Edwardian gentleman of conservative views. As such, he provided a stark contrast with many artists of the day. The dominant personality in the world of painting was Walter Sickert, a bohemian figure whose embrace of stark realism brought him closer in spirit to the era's novelists. His unflinching portrayal of the seamier side of London life reached a peak in a sequence of paintings called 'The Camden Town Murder', which drew their inspiration from a real-life cause célèbre – the killing of a prostitute called Emily Dimmock in seedy lodgings in north London. The subject was shocking at the time, the more so for its brutal contrast with the idealised classicism of late Victorian academic art. Sickert attracted around him a group of like-minded artists, including Spencer Gore and Robert Bevan, who collectively became known as the Fitzroy Street Group after Sickert's home address – a precursor of the later Camden Town Group, formed from the same circle's ranks.

One note largely missing from the Edwardian art scene was modernism, which was beginning to attract attention on the Continent via the music of Stravinsky (his 'Firebird' was premièred in Paris in 1910) and the paintings of Matisse and the group known as *Les Fauves* (the 'wild beasts'). Some of their work finally got a showing in a pioneering exhibition staged at London's Grafton Gallery by art critic Roger Fry in 1910. Their works hung alongside paintings by Cézanne, Gauguin and Van Gogh – all virtually unknown in Britain at the time. Seeking a label to unite the various artists, Fry and his colleagues came up with 'Post-Impressionist', and the name stuck.

Fry's exhibition was controversial at the time, and many of the people who crowded in to see it came only to scoff. The poet Wilfrid Scawen Blunt called the show 'pornographic', comparing the works to graffiti on toilet walls, while a doctor-critic published an article claiming that the artists involved were clinically insane. Even so, the exhibition was a harbinger of things to come and it got people talking about the modernist trend in art as never before.

CONTRASTING ATTITUDES
The Edwardian art world spanned a spectrum ranging from the conservatism of the writer Rudyard Kipling and composer Sir Edward Elgar (above) to the raffish bohemianism of such painters as Augustus John and Jack B Yeats (below). The son of a Worcester music dealer, Elgar married the daughter of a major-general and lived the life of a country gentleman. At the time of Elgar's greatest success, Yeats – the brother of the poet W B Yeats – was working in obscurity, drawing inspiration from childhood memories of the countryside around Sligo in Ireland. He developed a highly individual Expressionist style. The playwright Samuel Beckett was an admirer, writing of him '… he brings light, as only the great dare to bring light, to the issueless predicament of existence'.

SUMMER'S END

Within months of Campbell-Bannerman's election victory of 1906, it was all too apparent that the Prime Minister was a sick man. Before the end of the year he had the first of a series of heart attacks, and from November 1907 he was virtually incapacitated. He died on 22 April, 1908, just 17 days after resigning as Prime Minister. The social reform programme that he had done so much to put into practice would forge ahead and old age pensions became a reality before the end of the decade. But there was one area where Parliament proved reluctant to act: despite growing protest, the government refused to extend the vote to women.

CHAMPION SWIMMER Henry Taylor after his victory in the 400m freestyle event at the 1908 London Olympics – one of three gold medals he won at the games.

THE PEOPLE'S BUDGET

When Henry Campbell-Bannerman resigned as Liberal Prime Minister, on 5 April, 1908, there was never much doubt as to who would succeed him. H H Asquith (his Christian names, Herbert Henry, were rarely used) had already established himself as the party's safest pair of hands.

Asquith came from a middle-class commercial background in Yorkshire, but his childhood had been complicated by his father's death when he was just 7 years old. His natural ability won him a scholarship to Balliol College, Oxford, and he subsequently embarked on a successful law career. He won the attention of the ageing Gladstone through his intelligence and eloquence, and was unexpectedly made Home Secretary in the Grand Old Man's final Cabinet when still only 39. Throughout his career Asquith had an impressive ability to make impromptu speeches; when asked to reveal his notes for an address in support of the Licensing Bill of 1908, he produced a scrap of paper bearing the words 'Too many pubs'.

Asquith was Chancellor of the Exchequer when Campbell-Bannerman stepped down. The King was recuperating in Biarritz at the time, and so the new Prime Minister had to travel to France to receive the royal assent to his promotion. Inheriting a packed programme of reform, he quickly gave it fresh momentum by bringing forward a policy that he himself had helped to shape as Chancellor. This was the plan to introduce state pensions for the elderly poor.

The state pension and other social benefits

The business of managing the legislation to bring in the new pension devolved to the radically minded David Lloyd George, Asquith's successor at the Exchequer. To replace Lloyd George as President of the Board of Trade, Asquith chose another rising young talent: Winston Churchill. Between them, the two would be the main drivers of a new raft of social reforms. The measures introduced in the Pensions Act of 1908 were limited in scope, at least in the light of what was to follow. Men and women over the age of 70, with an annual income less than £31.50, received up to 5 shillings (25p) a week for a single person or 7 shillings 6 pence (37.5p) for married couples. To qualify, recipients had to have worked 'to their full potential' and to have lived in the country for at least 20 years.

No-one doubted the long-term significance of the legislation: the state was taking on a new level of responsibility for the well-being of its least well-off citizens. Traditional Tory opinion was shocked by the move. Lord Lansdowne, who had been Foreign Secretary under Balfour, commented that public money had been better spent on the Boer War, which raised the moral fibre of the country, than on state pensions, which weakened it. For beneficiaries, however, the money was an unalloyed blessing, providing a degree of financial security in their final years. In *Lark Rise to Candleford*, Flora Thompson recalled how recipients in her Oxfordshire village reacted: 'At first when they went to the Post Office to draw [the pension], tears of gratitude would run down the cheeks of some, and they would say as they picked up their money, "God bless that Lloyd George".'

While the Chancellor was busy with pensions, Churchill was pushing through important new measures at the Board of Trade. In 1909 he brought in labour

REFORMIST LEADER
H H Asquith took over as Liberal Prime Minister following Sir Henry Campbell-Bannerman's resignation. Asquith had been a successful barrister before he became a politician and he brought a clear legal mind and forensic debating skills to the Commons. He steered his party to victory in two general elections and was to hold office for eight years, the longest term of any 20th-century premier until Margaret Thatcher in the 1980s. Yet his time in power was marked by confrontation and crises, first in the domestic arena and latterly with the outbreak of the First World War.

'GOD BLESS LLOYD GEORGE'

State pensions were not a novel idea in 1908; at least ten other countries had already introduced them, notably Britain's main industrial rival, Germany. British workers without financial means still faced the prospect of either dependence on their families or the workhouse in old age. That situation changed with the Pensions Act steered through by Chancellor David Lloyd George in August 1908. Even though the sums paid out were low, they brought a degree of financial security to people like these elderly London ladies, seen enjoying a day trip to Epping Forest. Soon advertisers caught on (right) and began promoting their products as an aid to longevity.

OLD AGE PENSIONERS
DARBY—"A Happy New Year, my dear. Thanks to OXO we've got the pensions and thanks to OXO we'll enjoy them another 30 Years."

exchanges to help unemployed workers find jobs. He also introduced minimum wages in certain 'sweated' industries, where people worked in poor conditions for low pay. Ironically, the reforms were poorly received by the people they were intended to help: the labour movement regarded them with suspicion, fearing particularly that the trade boards might cost jobs and reduce the unions' power to maintain pay differentials between groups of workers.

Demand for Dreadnoughts

Meanwhile, the measures had to be paid for, a task that was further complicated by demands for money from a very different source. In the years since 1900 Britain had been involved in a naval armaments race with Germany. When Kaiser Wilhelm II's government took steps to double the size of the German fleet, Britain's First Sea Lord, Sir John Fisher, argued vociferously for increased outlay on the Royal Navy. In particular Fisher wanted more state-of-the-art, turbine-powered battleships like the prototype *Dreadnought* launched in 1906. The Conservative opposition in the Commons and the Northcliffe press both took up the call, coining the slogan 'We want eight and we won't wait'.

Faced with the growing clamour, the government agreed to lay down four more vessels, with a further four authorised for 1910. The decision placed an unprecedented strain on the nation's finances, which were already burdened by the cost of the new pensions. Casting around for new revenue sources, Lloyd George made the fateful decision to place the burden squarely on the shoulders of the rich. His 'People's Budget' of 1909 increased taxes on incomes above £3,000 a year, raised death duties and the tariffs on tobacco and spirits, and, most controversially of all, introduced new taxes on land, including a 20 per cent levy on unearned rises in the value of estates.

Revolt by the Lords

Lloyd George's proposals directly targeted the land-owning classes, who not surprisingly rose in revolt against them. The Chancellor justified his measures in a speech proclaiming that the 'sole function and chief pride' of his opponents was 'the stately consumption of wealth produced by others'. They responded by organising a Budget Protest League to coordinate resistance outside Parliament. The House of Lords, representing the landed vote in its purest form, prepared to do battle. Although a long-established convention prevented the Upper House from voting down finance bills approved by the Commons, their Lordships were in no mood for compromise and turned out in force. Margot Asquith, the Prime Minister's wife, later recalled that when the budget came to a vote that November, 'aged peers came from remote regions of the countryside who could not even find their way to the Houses of Parliament'. In a direct challenge to the authority of the government, the bill was rejected in the House of Lords by a majority of 225. Asquith had no alternative but to dissolve parliament and go to the country.

The election that ensued in January 1910 saw the highest voter turnout in British electoral history – 86.6 per cent. The result was a hung parliament; the Conservatives with their Liberal Unionist allies won the largest share of the vote, but the Liberals won two seats more than the Conservatives. They clung to power with the support of Labour and the Irish Nationalists. In the constitutional deadlock that followed, Asquith confronted the Lords head-on, threatening to create 500 new Liberal peers to overcome the built-in Conservative majority in the

NAVAL RACE
Britain's naval rivalry with Germany was the first and perhaps the greatest of a series of costly arms races that would sap the nation's economic strength over the course of the 20th century. It got under way with a misunderstanding, when Royal Navy seamen boarded a German mail steamer in 1900 in the mistaken belief that it was carrying arms to the Boers. Although the Admiralty apologised, the authorities in Berlin used the incident to bring in a Navy Law doubling the size of the German fleet. Britain felt obliged to respond in kind, regarding naval supremacy as essential for the survival of its far-flung empire. The race stepped up when Sir John Fisher (above) became First Sea Lord in 1904. Condemning 150 existing ships as unfit for service, he set about replacing them with new vessels. The pride of the fleet were the Dreadnoughts, named for the eponymous turbine-powered battleship (right) whose guns were capable of delivering a barrage of 6,800lb – more than 3 tonnes – of high explosives.

BECOMING HOUSEHOLD NAMES

Destined to become a giant of the British high street, Marks and Spencer traces its origins to a single open-market stall in Leeds run by Michael Marks, an immigrant from Minsk in what was then imperial Russia. Marks gradually expanded the business to covered markets, like the stall above, first in Leeds and then in towns across Yorkshire and Lancashire, advertising his goods under the slogan, 'Don't Ask the Price, It's a Penny'. In 1894, needing extra capital to fund further growth, Marks went into partnership with Thomas Spencer, chief cashier for the wholesale distribution firm that provided much of his merchandise. More branches followed and by 1903, when the business became a limited company, the number had grown to over 60.

John Sainsbury had opened his first shop in 1869 in Drury Lane, London, selling fresh foods. Packaged groceries were not added until 1903 when the rapidly growing business purchased a grocery store in Dalston. By the early 1920s, Sainsbury was the largest grocery chain in the country.

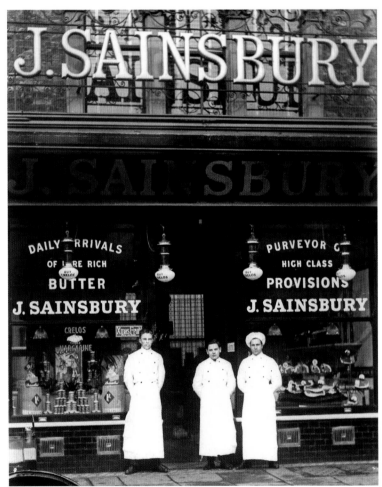

Upper House. First Edward VII and then, after his death, the new king George V unwillingly agreed to back him. The crisis soon led to yet another election, in December 1910, which shrank the Liberal lead over the Conservatives to just one seat. The issue was finally resolved through the Parliament Act of 1911, by which the House of Lords agreed, under substantial duress, to limit its own powers: henceforth, it would only be able to delay measures approved by the Commons, not veto them entirely. The Commons thereby confirmed the ascendancy that was its due in a democratic society – but at a lasting cost. The bitterness aroused by the constitutional crisis fed through to society at large, contributing to a wave of social unrest that swept the country in the years leading up to the First World War and, in the long term, to the demise of the Liberals as a party of government.

VOTES FOR WOMEN

SPREADING THE WORD
The cause of votes for women was a familiar one by the year 1900, but it gained huge momentum in the Edwardian years. Much of the publicity was generated by the Women's Social and Political Union, set up by Emmeline Pankhurst in 1903. From the start the WSPU adopted a confrontational approach that kept the movement in the headlines, attracting support and hostility in almost equal measure. Even among its supporters its methods were sometimes controversial. The Women's Freedom League, seen campaigning below, was set up by breakaway WSPU members who became disillusioned with what they saw as the movement's autocratic leadership. In particular, they took issue with the decision to cancel the annual conference and leave decision-making instead to a central committee nominated by Mrs Pankhurst and her daughter Christabel.

By 1908 another democratic cause was making its presence felt across the nation, and it too was proving bitterly divisive. The women's suffrage movement had gathered momentum through the last decades of Victoria's reign, spawning a bewildering variety of organisations all devoted to the cause of winning the right to vote. In an attempt to establish some sort of unity, the National Union of Women's Suffrage Societies (NUWSS) was set up in 1897 as an umbrella group to co-ordinate their efforts. The new body made progress through the 1900s, and by 1909 more than 200 individual groups were affiliated to it.

Yet it was another, very different group that made the headlines for much of that time. The Women's Social and Political Union (WSPU) first saw the light of day in Manchester in 1903. While the NUWSS promoted democratic decision-making, the WSPU was run autocratically by its charismatic founder, Emmeline Pankhurst, who operated largely through an unelected central committee. And while most NUWSS affiliates adopted a course of patient advocacy, Mrs Pankhurst's group chose the path of confrontation.

Seismic changes had been going on beneath the surface of late-Victorian society and the idea that women should be confined to the traditional roles of wife, mother, servant or governess, was increasingly under fire. Although domestic service remained the main career path for working-class girls, other opportunities had become available, particularly in the northern textile mills. There were also increasing numbers of so-called 'white-blouse' jobs in offices, shops and schools. Before the 1870 Education Act, for example, there had been only 14,000 teachers in the whole of England, two-thirds of them male; by 1900 there were 100,000 teachers and three-quarters of them were women. Like Hilda Lessways in Arnold Bennett's *Clayhanger*, middle-class women were gaining a degree of financial independence by putting typewriting skills and knowledge of the Pitman shorthand system to use in business.

By 1900 women's growing economic power had brought about some social and political progress. Through the board schools almost all girls were now literate and numerate, and pressure from women's groups had achieved some advances in respect of property rights within marriage. There had

'Never had I imagined that so many people could be gathered together to share in a political demonstration.'

Emmeline Pankhurst, writing on the Women's Sunday rally held in Hyde Park on 2 June, 1908

MASS MOVEMENT

By the latter part of the decade the suffragette cause had become a mass movement. One of the main ways of spreading the message was through public meetings and rallies like this one in Trafalgar Square (left). Speakers at such rallies – here a Mrs Baines from Stockport – did not always find themselves preaching to the converted; often they had to face light-hearted banter and sometimes verbal abuse or even the threat of violence. Mrs Pankhurst became renowned for the cool-headedness with which she dealt with such unwanted interruptions; when Oxford undergraduates once tried to disturb her in mid-speech by releasing a mouse onto the platform, she simply picked the creature up and stroked it.

By 1907 the campaign had gained a big enough following to permit Mrs Pankhurst to devote all her time to campaigning. The extent of the support became obvious the following year when the Women's Social and Political Union called a mass demonstration in Hyde Park. Held on Sunday 21 June – Women's Sunday, as the WSPU christened it – the rally attracted several hundred thousand people, brought to London from all parts of the country in specially commissioned trains. Seven separate processions, of which this is one (right), converged on the Park from different directions, and speakers made the case for the franchise from 20 different platforms – efficient electrical amplification had not yet been invented. Mrs Pankhurst would later write: 'When I mounted my platform in Hyde Park, and surveyed the mighty throngs that waited there and the endless crowds that were still pouring into the park from all directions, I was filled with amazement not unmixed with awe. Never had I imagined that so many people could be gathered together to share in a political demonstration.'

even been a few political gains: single or widowed rate-payers had been able to vote in local elections from as early as 1869, and the right was extended to married women in 1894. In this respect the Isle of Man was way ahead of the game, for Manx women had been given a voice in voting for the island's parliament, the House of Keys, in 1881.

Injustice and inequality

Such achievements paled in feminist eyes beside the work that still remained to be done. Women may have had increasing access to the workplace, but their wages averaged barely two-thirds those of men. Despite the progress made in improving the status of wives, inequalities still existed in the divorce laws, which permitted only husbands to cite adultery as grounds for separation. Above all, British women were expected to pay taxes, but as they were still denied a voice in government they had no say in how those taxes were raised or spent.

The right to vote became the focus of discontent, and Emmeline Pankhurst took up the role of standard-bearer of the suffragette struggle. She inherited her dramatic flair and taste for extravagant gestures from her father, a self-made Manchester businessman who was also the city's leading amateur actor. Educated locally and at the École Normale in Paris, Emmeline married a prominent radical barrister and the two threw themselves into a variety of progressive causes. They also had five children, two of them boys who died in infancy. Of the girls, Christabel and Sylvia took a prominent part in the suffrage movement.

Following her husband's death in 1898, Emmeline was forced by economic circumstances to take a salaried job as a registrar of births and deaths. She saved most of her considerable energy, however, for the WSPU, which was founded at a

PRISON ORDEAL
By the end of the decade a jail term had become something of a badge of honour for militant suffragettes prepared to take direct action to achieve their goals. In 1908 Emmeline and Christabel Pankhurst (left) were sentenced to three months in London's Holloway Prison for issuing a proclamation that was considered seditious. Emmeline, who had already served a six-week term earlier that year, was disgusted by the damp, the cockroaches and the insanitary conditions in the prison, as well as by the 'hideous prison dress stamped all over with the broad arrow of disgrace'. Yet she regarded her suffering as a good way of drawing attention to the cause. She was to be arrested seven times over the next six years, telling the court on one occasion: 'We are here not because we are law-breakers; we are here in our efforts to become law-makers.' Many other militants followed her example, among them Emmeline Pethick-Lawrence (right), seen emerging triumphantly from a 1909 prison term to the plaudits of well-wishers. Pethick-Lawrence was at the time a loyal lieutenant of the Pankhursts, serving as treasurer of the WSPU and, with her lawyer husband, running its journal, *Votes for Women*. When the couple subsequently dared to express reservations about the WSPU's adoption of violent methods, Mrs Pankhurst expelled them from the movement.

meeting in her home. The group's first act of militancy came in 1905, when a private member's bill in favour of women's suffrage was talked out in the Commons. Emmeline and her followers noisily protested and were duly expelled from the House. Five months later Christabel and a working-class militant, Annie Kenney, interrupted a speech by the Liberal statesman Sir Edward Grey at Manchester's Free Trade Hall; they were arrested when Christabel spat at a policeman. Refusing to pay the fines imposed on them, the two ended up serving short prison sentences. In the wake of the affair the *Daily Mail*, no friend of the cause, christened the WSPU militants 'suffragettes', seeking thereby to distinguish them from the more moderate 'suffragists' of the NUWSS.

The intensity of the WSPU campaign steadily escalated. Emmeline herself first went to prison in 1908, when she refused to be bound over after leading a protest march on Parliament. That year also witnessed the largest political demonstration seen up till then in Britain: an estimated half a million people, brought in from all over the country on 30 special trains, attended a rally for the cause in Hyde Park.

Then, too, the first attacks on property began, when radical suffragettes threw stones at windows of 10 Downing Street. That October, Emmeline was back in prison, along with her daughter Christabel, sentenced to three months each for issuing a handbill urging their followers to 'rush the House of Commons'.

By 1909 WSPU members were regularly harassing cabinet ministers. Some of those imprisoned for their acts went on hunger strike to draw further attention to their cause. The authorities responded by ordering the women to be force-fed, a humiliating and painful procedure that involved forcing a tube up the prisoner's nose and down into the throat. Such oppressive measures stimulated responses that sometimes bordered on the hysterical; one aristocratic detainee, Lady Constance Lytton, tried to tattoo the words 'Votes for Women' on her chest with a needle. By 1910 patience over the issue was wearing very thin indeed. The lack of action on the part of the government would trigger an explosion of anger from activists that dwarfed the confrontations of the Edwardian decade.

SPORT TURNS PROFESSIONAL

SPORTING GIANT
C B Fry poses with his friend and colleague Kumar Shri Ranjitsinhji, who played alongside him in the Sussex and England cricket teams. Fry was a multi-talented athlete who also excelled at soccer, rugby and athletics. In cricket he headed the national batting averages six times, on one occasion in 1901 scoring centuries in six successive innings. 'Ranji' – an Indian prince who had played little cricket before going up to Cambridge University – was also regarded as one of the finest batsmen of his day, amassing over 3000 runs in the 1899 and 1900 seasons and captaining Sussex from 1899 to 1903. He later became the Maharajah of Nawanagar and after the First World War he represented India at the League of Nations.

For light relief in a time of strife and economic recession the public flocked to spectator sports, which drew unprecedented crowds in the years to 1910. Cricket was enjoying a golden age, bequeathing for posterity a lingering image of village greens on summer afternoons echoing to the reassuring thud of willow on leather. The decade was a great time for the amateur game, played by teams with colourful names like 'I Zingari' or the 'Free Foresters'.

Professional cricket was also well established: the County Championship had been in operation since 1889, and full-time salaried players formed the backbone of the 16 sides that now took part . Up to 30,000 spectators turned out to watch Yorkshire playing at home on a sunny day. The great W G Grace retired from the game in 1900, but other giants soon came forward to take his place. Gilbert Jessop of Gloucestershire was a famous big hitter, reckoned by some authorities to have been the fastest run-scorer in cricketing history. And in the remarkable C B Fry England found the Edwardian era's successor to Grace.

A gifted popular hero

Fry was an Oxford scholar, said to have been a match for the best minds of his generation, who went on to become the only person ever to represent England at cricket (and to captain the national side) and also to play in an FA Cup Final (in the Southampton team that lost to Sheffield United in 1902). He played rugby for Blackheath and the Barbarians, and in athletics was for a time the joint world record-holder in the long-jump. Legend has it that he was supple enough to do a backflip from a standing position and land on a mantelpiece behind him.

For all his many sporting talents, Fry remained an amateur throughout his playing career, earning his keep first as a schoolteacher and later as the

UP FOR THE CUP
Dressed in their Sunday best, Everton fans in London for the 1906 FA Cup Final take a break on their way to watch the match. They would have been celebrating later that evening, for their team won by a single goal scored 13 minutes from time by their centre forward, Alex 'Sandy' Young. The result was a bitter blow for the Newcastle supporters, who had seen their team lose the final to Aston Villa the year before. The game was played before 75,000 spectators at the Crystal Palace ground, home to FA Cup Final matches from 1895 to 1914.

commander of a Royal Navy training vessel. He wrote several books and was persuaded by the publisher George Newnes to lend his name to *C B Fry's Magazine*, a sports and adventure monthly. In later life Fry became somewhat eccentric, suffering periods of mental instability in which he was sometimes seen running naked along Brighton beach. One of his odder ventures was a quixotic attempt in the 1930s to persuade Hitler's Germany to take up cricket to test level. Earlier, he had been briefly sounded out as a possible candidate for the vacant Albanian throne. Stephen Fry claims to be one of his descendants.

The professional game

While brilliant amateurs like C B Fry continued to illuminate British sport, the way of the future lay with the professional game. The point was brought home most clearly by soccer, which benefited hugely from the increased leisure time and spending power of the working men who flocked through the turnstiles, particularly in the northern half of the country. Real wages of skilled and semi-skilled workers had risen by an estimated 30 per cent in the decades since 1870, and it was increasingly common for employees to clock off at noon on Saturdays, leaving the afternoons free for supporting the local team.

The Football League had got under way in 1888, with a Second Division added in 1892. The clubs were established as limited companies, but they rarely made profits that were not ploughed back into the game. To keep costs down, the authorities imposed a maximum wage for players of £4 a week, about twice the sum earned by a well-paid factory worker. There was also a £10 limit on signing-on fees, but the amount paid for transfers was not capped. The most successful clubs used this loophole to attract the best players: the £1,000 barrier was first breached in 1905, when the England striker Alf Common moved from Sunderland to Middlesbrough.

The game that the fans now flocked to see was recognisably the same one played today, although with some noticeable differences. In the early 1900s, for example, players still wore knickerbockers reaching down to the knee rather than shorts, although the obligation to do so was removed in 1905. By that time clubs were providing gyms for their squad to work out in and were employing trainers

TAKING THE LEAD
Harry Hampton (third from left) scores for Aston Villa after just two minutes of the 1905 Cup Final, while Newcastle United defenders look helplessly on. Villa went on to win the match 2–0, with Hampton scoring again in the 76th minute. Teams from the Midlands and North continued to dominate the competition through much of the Edwardian era, although Tottenham Hotspur were shock winners in 1901, delighting a record crowd of over 114,000, swollen by the presence of a London club in the Final. The burgeoning number of spectators was an indicator of soccer's fast-growing popularity; just 2,000 fans had turned out for the first cup final, held at the Oval in 1872.

STAYING COMPETITIVE

One sign of the growing professionalism of soccer was the development of the league game, which by the turn of the century was well established in Scotland as well as England. Queen's Park, Scotland's oldest football club, finally agreed to join the Scottish League in 1900, having previously objected to the fact that players could be paid for their services. The Glasgow team Third Lanark (above) was a founder member. They were league champions in 1904 and remained top-level competitors until the 1960s before collapsing into bankruptcy in 1967.

Another sign of the times on both sides of the border was the hiring of trainers and masseurs to keep players match-fit. To judge by this photograph of two Newcastle United players working out with Indian clubs and a chest expander, physical fitness regimes were rather less sophisticated than they are today.

to give them rubdowns. Supporters were quite as partisan as today, wearing club rosettes and shaking rattles, and there were lots of them: the average First Division fixture attracted a 15,000 gate, while the 1901 Cup Final, staged at Crystal Palace, drew a staggering 114,815 attendance. One reason for the record crowd was the fact that a London team, Tottenham Hotspur, had reached the final, a feat matched by only two other London clubs before the First World War. Soccer remained very much the northern game that it had been when the League was first set up with a dozen participants – none of them from further south than Derby.

A Scottish league had also been established with 11 teams in 1890, and there too the game attracted passionate enthusiasm. One of the first major sporting disasters occurred at the Ibrox Park stadium in Glasgow in 1902, when part of the stand collapsed under the weight of spectators watching the annual Scotland–England international match; 26 people were killed and over 500 injured. Scotland also saw one of the earliest soccer riots, at Hampden Park in 1909, when a Celtic–Rangers Scottish Cup Final ended in a draw and the authorities decided to arrange a replay rather than settle the issue in extra time.

For all soccer's growing professionalism, it was still possible for the best amateur clubs to take on First Division opposition and win. Corinthians proved the point memorably in 1903 by beating Bury 10–3 shortly after the League side had won the FA Cup without conceding a goal in the entire campaign.

continued on page 154

THE LONDON OLYMPICS

The 1908 Olympics were not originally destined for London. They had been assigned to Rome, but an eruption of Mount Vesuvius in 1906 required such a costly relief effort that the Italian government pulled out on financial grounds. With just two years in which to prepare, the organisers took advantage of a major event already planned for 1908: the Franco-British Exhibition. Happy to draw extra spectators, the exhibition authorities agreed to build a 66,000-seater stadium on their site at White City in west London. All the work was completed on time and, with the City toastmaster (right) in attendance to make announcements, the Games were ready to begin.

ON WITH THE SHOW

From the start the Games were dogged by controversy. The organisers failed to display the US flag in the stadium, and in response the flagbearer of the US team refused to dip the Stars and Stripes, as custom demanded, when marching past the royal box. The bad feeling continued into the competition. When a US runner was adjudged to have deliberately impeded the British favourite in the 400m final, the race was declared void and the offender disqualified. The other two finalists, both from the USA, refused to take part in the re-run, so the British athlete became the only person ever to win Olympic gold by a walkover.

But despite such niggles and the rainy July weather, the Games soon got the nation's attention. The Marathon was a highlight, run for the first time over its present length of 26 miles 385 yards (40.6km), the planned 25-mile route having been lengthened to start at Windsor Castle. Competitors had to provide a certificate of fitness to enter and were examined by the Games' own doctors (left). The Italian Dorando Pietri was leading on entering the stadium, but was in the final stages of exhaustion; after collapsing several times, he was helped to the finish line by sympathetic officials. As a result he was disqualified, but his courage had so impressed the crowd that he was awarded a special cup by Queen Alexandra.

Another reason for the popularity of the Games was the success of home athletes. The cycling pursuit team (above) won gold, while Walter Tysall from Birmingham (right) took silver in the individual gymnastics. In all, the British claimed 146 medals, well ahead of second-placed USA with 47.

CROWD PLEASERS

The Games featured several events that were later dropped from the Olympic schedule. One such was the tug-of-war (top left), contested from 1900 to 1920. Participation was open to clubs rather than national teams, meaning that several from one country could enter; in 1908 all three medals went to British police outfits, including the Liverpool squad shown in action, which won silver.

Archery was dropped in 1920, but was reinstated in 1972 and is still regularly contested. The women's event in 1908 (bottom left) attracted only home entrants, ensuring that British competitors swept the medals. The victor was 53-year-old Sybil 'Queenie' Newall from Rochdale, the oldest woman ever to win Olympic gold.

Fears that the Games might not prove a success soon proved unfounded, although not before the poor weather caused some initial qualms. To stimulate interest, celebrities were invited to attend – the biggest draw was Maud Allan, an exotic dancer whose daring performance of the Dance of the Seven Veils from Oscar Wilde's play *Salome* was the hit of the London season. Thereafter, the stadium was regularly filled to capacity. These spectators (right) are celebrating the victory of 19-year-old Reggie Walker of South Africa in the 100m final; he beat three North American rivals to take gold.

In all, 2008 athletes from 22 nations participated in 110 separate events. Only 37 competitors were women, all of them archers, ice-skaters or tennis players.

The amateur–professional divide was more marked in rugby, where it caused a schism that survives to this day. In 1895 the Rugby Football Union had determined to retain the amateur principle by banning clubs that charged spectators entrance fees and paid their players. But the Northern Union needed the gate money to support the working men who made up most of its teams, and so broke away. In the 1900s the split between rugby union and rugby league became entrenched as rule changes drove an enduring wedge between the two traditions. From 1906 on, rugby league teams were reduced in size from 15 to 13 players; at the same time a new regulation permitted players brought down while holding the ball to retain possession by back-heeling it to another member of the side. The aim was to reduce the number of loose rucks and mauls and so encourage a more open, mobile game that would please the watching crowds.

The split that opened up in rugby football's ranks in a sense epitomised the north–south divide that continued to mark the country as a whole, just as it had throughout Queen Victoria's reign. Yet there was one sport that was not only truly national in its scope but also managed to appeal to all social classes. This was horse-racing, which thoroughly earned its nickname of the Sport of Kings from the patronage it received from Edward VII. Horses owned by Edward started the decade by winning the Derby and Grand National in 1900, and ended it winning the Derby again in 1909. His most successful year was 1902, when his filly Sceptre won the Grand Slam of the St Leger, the Oaks, and the 1000 and 2000 Guineas.

BRITAIN'S PLACE IN THE WORLD

As the first decade of the 20th century drew to a close, one man put his mind to taking stock of the years since Victoria's passing. Charles Masterman, a progressive Liberal MP and grand-nephew of the prison reformer Elizabeth Fry, published *The Condition of England* in 1909. A major area of concern, for Masterman and others, was the fear that Britain was being outpaced both industrially and technologically by its overseas competitors.

The decade had seen aviation pioneered in the USA and France, while Germany had come to the fore in motor engineering – at least until Henry Ford developed the techniques of mass production that would establish US predominance. Even in shipbuilding, long a British strength, the Germans were making advances; ocean liners built in German shipyards had won the prestigious Blue Riband for the fastest Atlantic crossing in three successive years, from 1904 to 1906. Only in 1907 did the turbine-powered *Lusitania* re-establish Britain's hold. British industry had success stories – chemicals were thriving, and by 1911 mechanical and electrical engineering were employing twice as many workers as iron and steel – but these were too often outshone by the progress being made in other countries.

Like many of his contemporaries, Masterman was also concerned that Britain was falling demographically behind its main rival, Germany. 'The headlong

WHITE CITY WONDERLAND
The Franco-British Exhibition that ended up hosting the 1908 Olympic Games was a lavish monument to the spirit of friendship between the two nations in the wake of the Entente Cordiale. It was the largest such event since the Great Exhibition of 1851, occupying a 140 acre (57 hectare) site at Shepherds Bush that would thereafter be known as White City from the colour of the exhibition buildings. The attractions on display included the Flip-Flap (top right), a precursor of the London Eye offering panoramic views over the city, and the Court of Honour, where visitors could admire the Indian-style architecture from pedal-powered Swan Boats (bottom right) or from electric launches. After dark the Court of Honour (overleaf) was lit up by 160,000 lightbulbs in a spectacular demonstration of the power of electricity.

Among the other highlights of the exhibition were the Irish and Senegalese villages, designed to illustrate life in different corners of the empire. The Irish village was staffed by 150 'colleens' demonstrating handicrafts. The exhibition ran from mid-May until the end of October, attracting a total of over 8 million paying spectators, with the Olympic Games taking place in July. The site on which the exhibition stood is now occupied by the BBC Television Centre and the Westfield shopping precinct.

collapse of the birth rate of this country – a fall greater than in any other nation in Europe – is a phenomenon to which all the classes, save the very poorest, are probable contributors', he wrote. The decline was only comparative, for the population of the mainland in fact grew by almost 4 million over the course of the decade to a total of 40.5 million. But the rate of increase was down, and this fact combined with a decline in the number of deaths to signal an ageing population.

The effects were particularly marked in the countryside, where the continuing drift to the cities contributed to a sense of decay. By the end of the decade only 8 per cent of the workforce worked on the land, and people were increasingly aware that Britain had become an urban nation. In Masterman's words: 'The little red-roofed towns and hamlets, the labourer in the fields at noontide or evening, the old English service in the old English village church, now stand but as the historical survival of a once great and splendid past.' The Britain of 1910 belonged more and more to the middle-class residents of the cities and suburbs, who were increasingly challenging the right of the landed aristocracy to run the country.

Red-brick rise

One reason for the rise of the middle classes lay in the educational revolution that had begun in 1870 and gathered pace since Balfour's Education Act of 1902. The Edwardian years saw rapid expansion of higher education. Birmingham University got its royal charter in 1900, and existing colleges in Sheffield and Bristol acquired full university status in 1905 and 1909 respectively. This initial roll call of what became known as the 'red-brick' universities was completed by the conferral of independent status on the three constituent parts of the existing Victoria University, respectively as the universities of Manchester, Liverpool and Leeds.

Architecturally the decade was more marked by private residences, built by the likes of Edwin Lutyens and Charles Rennie Mackintosh, than by large-scale public commissions. Masterman deplored the shortage of the latter, claiming they were limited to 'a Byzantine cathedral at Westminster, a Gothic cathedral at Liverpool, a few town halls and libraries of sober solidity [and] the white buildings which today line Whitehall'. House-building was a recurrent theme in literature, whether in the shape of Forsyte's new Surrey mansion in Galsworthy's *Man of Property*, the Howard's End of E M Foster's novel of that name, or the new family home that plays a central part in Arnold Bennett's *Clayhanger*. The house represented more than a bricks-and-mortar statement of social status: it stood for a way of putting down roots in a society increasingly in flux.

For Britain was changing fast throughout Edward's reign. On the surface the upper classes maintained the starched formality and decorum of the previous century, as though to proclaim that life in the capital of empire was rolling on majestically much as it had always done. If anything, the Edwardian upper classes added a touch of showiness to the older traditions and a flaunting of new wealth. Yet fresh forces were making themselves felt, whether in the fierce rhetoric of the suffragettes demanding rights for women or the intellectual 'anything-goes' of the emergent Bloomsbury Group, who would come to the fore in the following decade. And if the middle classes were finding their voice politically, then so too were the workers, whose vehicle, the Labour Party, would eclipse the reformist Liberals before a dozen years were out. In retrospect the Edwardian decade would come to seem like a golden summer, but all too soon the glow would fade through a brief, troubled autumn into the savage winter of the First World War.

INDEX

PICTURE ACKNOWLEDGEMENTS

Abbreviations: t = top; m = middle; b = bottom; r = right; c = centre; l = left

All images in this book are courtesy of Getty Images, including the following which have additional attributions:
17, 25bl, 25br, 28, 36t, 37, 46, 52-3, 72r, 91, 96, 98, 101, 103t, 122t, 140, 146, 148-149, 151b, 153: Popperfoto
30, 49b, 82: Time & Life Pictures
38, 78, 80, 87: Sean Sexton
55: Roger Viollet
130 bl: George Eastman House

LOOKING BACK AT BRITAIN
EDWARDIAN SUMMER – 1900s
is published by The Reader's Digest Association Ltd,
London, in association with Getty Images and
Endeavour London Ltd.

Copyright © 2009 The Reader's Digest Association Ltd

The Reader's Digest Association Ltd
11 Westferry Circus
Canary Wharf
London E14 4HE
www.readersdigest.co.uk

Endeavour London Ltd
21–31 Woodfield Road
London W9 2BA
info@endeavourlondon.com

Written by
Tony Allan

For Endeavour
Publisher: Charles Merullo
Designer: Tea Aganovic
Picture editors: Jennifer Jeffrey, Franziska Payer Crockett
Production: Mary Osborne

For Reader's Digest
Project editor: Christine Noble
Art editor: Conorde Clarke
Indexer: Marie Lorimer
Proofreader: Ron Pankhurst
Pre-press account manager: Dean Russell
Product production manager: Claudette Bramble
Production controller: Sandra Fuller

Reader's Digest General Books
Editorial director: Julian Browne
Art director: Anne-Marie Bulat

Colour origination by Chroma Graphics Ltd, Singapore
Printed and bound in China

We are committed both to the quality of our
products and the service we provide to our customers.
We value your comments, so please do contact us on
08705 113366 or via our website at
www.readersdigest.co.uk

If you have any comments or suggestions about
the content of our books, email us at
gbeditorial@readersdigest.co.uk

CONCEPT CODE: UK 0154/L/S
BOOK CODE: 638-008 UP0000-1
ISBN: 978 0 276 44396 1
ORACLE CODE: 356900008H.00.24